Praise for
WILD & HOLY WOMEN
OF THE BIBLE

Please read this book. It isn't often that I speak so boldly about what someone else should do with their time but in the case of Sherry Cothran's book, *Wild and Holy Women of the Bible*, it feels less like an injunction and more like an emphatic 'this is what your soul has been waiting for' truth. I love this book! My copy is filled with highlights, underlines, and dog ears. These songs, reflections and questions helped me experience t way. Sherry is theologically brilli your perspective about what you single word to see vast new spiritu come into the light, rest, play, and ....tions to freedom that were birthed in Sherry's own spiritual wrestling have jumped off the page to become companions for me in my walk with Jesus.

Thoughts like: 'But often, we only think of resurrection as something that occurs in a Bible story. What if it could also happen to a Bible story?" And "What it is that I truly love?" You may have to ask this question a hundred times before you find an answer that fits. That's okay. Just keep asking."

Wild and Holy Women of the Bible is a book I'll be coming back to again and again. It is beautiful, invitational, and profound in its simplicity. And most importantly, it is deepening how I understand myself as a child of God and my work in the world. For your heart, your healing, and your very wholeness, read this book. Please, read this book.

Rev. Sarah Ciavarri, M.Div., BCC, PCC, CDTLF, CDWF-C
Author, *Finding Our Way to Truth: Seven Lies Leaders Believe and How to Let Them Go*, Fortress Press

Cothran revisits the women of the Old Testament with the intellectual skill of a first rate biblical scholar, and with the artistic and poetic insights of an outstanding songwriter. Her work is poetic, smart, devotional, and grounded deeply in her own faith and practice as a Christian minister. This is the best way imaginable to become immersed in these stories. After reading the biblical text, and hearing Cothran's song and creative interpretation, we experience each story woven into the fabric of our lives. We are not merely taught these stories, our lives are rescripted by them and the truths they so vividly express.

Rev. Dr. John S. McClure, Charles G. Finney Professor of
Preaching and Worship, Vanderbilt Divinity School, Author,
Mashup Religion: Pop Music and Theological Invention

In *Prophets, Warriors, Harlots & Healers: Wild and Holy Women of the Bible*, author Sherry Cothran leads the reader on a journey of encounter with unexpected biblical heroes. She raises up women's stories that lay buried in the Bible and only in recent decades have received attention from feminist scholars. From the warrior and prophet Deborah to the nameless daughter who became the victim to her father's heedless vow, Cothran lifts up voices that call to women today to rise up and "live our wild, holy and precious lives." Each chapter, on women's stories like Jael, Esther, Huldah and others, includes reflections on the wounds especially carried by women, traumas to their bodies and spirit, as illustrations of ways biblical women's presence in their communities create possibilities of healing for women today. The subtitle of the book "Leading Us on Healing Pathways" expresses the ultimate impact of considering these ancient stories. Each character is also present in a song that precedes the chapter devoted to her. These are written and performed by song-writer and singer Sherry Cothran in her inimitable style. The book and the songs are texts to sit with and contemplate with close attention. As the author puts it, "Go ahead, follow these women into the still-wild places of your very own heart. When you finally answer the call home, it will be sweeter than ever before."

Dr. Johanna W. H. van Wijk-Bos Professor of Old Testament Emerita
Louisville Presbyterian Theological Seminary

In her music and writing, Sherry Cothran guides us down a path of greater illumination. This is her true gift. Her work helps us see what we might have missed when we think about important characters and stories from the Bible. Too often, our focus is on Noah or Moses, Paul or the disciples, rather than on Huldah and Deborah, Rahab and the unnamed, but now not unknown, women of the Bible. Cothran shows that throughout the Bible, women are vital to telling the full story of God's interaction with God's people. This is a powerful vindication of the reality of women's experience and light for men who need to be liberated from the darkness of patriarchy.

Rev. Dr. Matthew W. Charlton,
Research Fellow, Stellenbosch University, South Africa and
Wesley House, Cambridge

As Sherry Cothran asserts and then goes on to demonstrate in her book, *Wild and Holy Women,* "We can learn new narratives from old stories." Weaving together ancient, often overlooked tales of unconventional women in the Bible with the modern female experience, Cothran helps us see meaningful connections and draw relevant insight for our own lives. This book is a compassionate and timely guide for women of faith who are discovering what it means to find—and use—their own voices to tell their own stories.

Staci Frenes, Songwriter and Author, *Love Makes Room,*
Broadleaf Books

Knowledge is power, so they say, and there is nothing more powerful than sharing knowledge that empowers us to live our best lives. As Rev. Sherry Cothran resurrects the stories of women that were buried beneath the rubble of patriarchy and misogyny, we find ourselves in their pain and their triumph. So shake off the dust on these centuries old stories, and raise the volume on voices that just may help us all arise.

Rev. N. Neelley Hicks
Exec. Director, Harper Hill Global & Women Arise Collective

PROPHETS, WARRIORS, HARLOTS & HEALERS:

WILD & HOLY WOMEN

OF THE BIBLE

Leading us on healing pathways.

SHERRY COTHRAN

SUNLAND
MEDIA

AN IMPRINT OF BELOVED WOMAN
A NONPROFIT CORPORATION

Published in Chattanooga, TN by Sunland Media.

Scripture quotations are from the New Revised Standard Version Bible, unless otherwise noted. 1989 Division of Christian Education of the National Council of Churches of Christ in the United States of America.

ISBN 979-0-578-24938-4 (Paperback)

LCCN 2021909514

For my husband, Patrick James Woolsey

Wild – *living in a state of nature and not ordinarily tame or domesticated*

Holy – *having a Divine nature*

CONTENTS

INTRODUCTION

"**S**he's not dead; she's only sleeping," Jesus exclaimed to a group of loud and boisterous mourners gathered to grieve the untimely death of Jairus' young daughter. He was stating the obvious; of course, she was only sleeping, at least to him. Death is not that final; that is, if you catch it soon enough. But instead of agreeing with him or expressing some anticipatory hope that this young girl might, indeed, live again, the story tells us that they laughed at him. They laughed at him! Really? Was resurrection funny in the ancient world? I mean, it wasn't that uncommon, there were rumors of those raised from the dead, legends and stories, and Jesus did, after all, have a reputation for the miraculous. Or was it, perhaps, laughable that a girl's life might be worth all the fuss? After all, the funeral party was well underway, and Jesus had been a latecomer. But instead of playing into their folly, he dismissed them. After the last befuddled person stumbled out of a room in which the aura of premature celebration still lingered, Jesus took a deep breath that settled into somber silence. He then lifted the young girl's limp and lifeless hand and said to her, "Talitha koum," which means, "Little Girl, rise up!" At which point, breath flowed back into her lungs, dreams pumped through her heart, and she rose to her feet and began to walk.

Resurrection. It's a powerful theme in the Bible. Dry bones put on flesh and dance, Lazarus rises after three days of death and walks out of the dark tomb foreshadowing Jesus' triumphant victory over the grave. The miracle of new life rising from what appears to be dead in the pages of the Bible is familiar to us. But often, we only think of resurrection as something that occurs *in* a Bible story. What if it could also happen *to* a Bible story?

For centuries, women's stories have lain buried in the Bible. But over the past few decades, female Bible scholars have been resurrecting them. As it turns out, the stories of female prophets, warriors, and heroic women of renown weren't dead; they were only sleeping. These wild and holy women of the Bible help us to untame traditional views of women and lead us on a healing journey with the Divine. Their voices call out to us all to rise up and live our wild, holy and precious lives.

The great burying of women's stories was well underway by the time Jesus invited an unnamed girl to "rise up." Jesus did his best to resurrect the women that his life touched. He was steeped in a history of strong women, born to one Mary with another Mary at his side. As a Jew, he was well acquainted with the stories that told of the "bravery of Esther and the fidelity of Ruth."[1] He even empowered women to follow him and fund his ministry out of their own money, Luke's gospel tells us, and become leaders in the early church movement. Although he radically altered women's lives, he couldn't change what was about to come. A great burying of the exquisite strength, power and wisdom displayed in the stories of so many women in this collection of books that would come to be known as the Holy Bible.

Even though the stories of the wild and holy women of the Bible seem hidden, the narrators of this sacred book felt compelled to leave them "as is." As Wilda Gafney so beautifully states, "…the biblical text presents female prophets leading the people of God and proclaiming the word of God unremarkably, as part of the natural order of things."[2] We'll explore this "natural order of things" as we come to see that these stories transform long-held traditional ideas. These wild and holy women of God were not created to be inferior to men and were not submissive or obedient to male authority. Still, God called them to take a sacred journey. Through their experiences, we can learn new narratives from old stories.

In this book, we'll meet the female prophets, warriors, and the harlot turned hero. We'll explore the untold story of an orphan queen and a queen who becomes a king. We'll visit a medium who becomes a truth-teller to a king. We'll explore these and other hidden treasures as we spin them into a golden thread and weave them into our tapestry of faith. We will see that this wild and holy woman of the Bible has been there all along, not dead, only sleeping. He story is waiting to rise up and come to life in us. Unbroken, whole, and free.

It's very likely that even if you are familiar with Bible stories, you may not have come across these stories before. Because we often see what we are taught to see. For a very long time, it seemed the early church fathers and male theologians of the middle ages had buried them quite successfully. These male founders of Christian theology from the first century and following chose selected scriptures to interpret, in their opinion, how God viewed women.[3] Their views of women seen through the constrained lens of a rigid patriarchal culture seemed iron-clad for centuries. Here are just a few of their ideas that became embedded in our cultural beliefs about women.

Women, they believed, were not created in the image of God; how could they be? They were inferior to men in their eyes, so something had to be missing. Tertullian thought that "women are the gate to hell…a temple built over a sewer,"[4] while Thomas Aquinas believed that women are "defective."[5] Augustine reasoned that since women weren't created in the image of God, the logical pathway for a woman to obtain wholeness was through her sexual union with a man.[6] These ideas may seem ludicrous to us now. Still, these oppressive beliefs about women reigned for centuries and became deeply rooted in our society.

These influential writings produced, over time, in many sects of the Christian church, the beliefs that shaped women's lives for centuries. Not only did the world become a dangerous place for a woman, but the Bible did, too. Instead of considering the vast range of women's roles in the sacred book that spanned over a millenia of the history of God's people, they presented a limited view of women and God. Their ideas became foundational in Christian practice. Which, of course, has produced a lot of human suffering for women and girls.

Through his global work in human rights, former President Jimmy Carter has found violence against women to be the most significant humanitarian issue of our time. He cites distorted interpretations of Scripture as the main underlying reason.[7] He has devoted himself to helping faith cultures understand that they are often unintentionally contributing to this violence through doctrine that supports derogatory beliefs about women. In our world today, violence against women thrives and has become institutionalized in many places. According to the World Health Organization and the United Nations, one in three women experience sexual or physical violence against them at some point in their lives.

Somehow, in this beautiful sacred book, we have learned to see restriction rather than freedom for women. We learned to see ourselves in the Bible's stories that portrayed women as subservient and submissive while the stories of women who led their communities, spoke God's Word, and became heroes were put to sleep. In doing so, we've placed restrictions on how God works through us in the world. How much more powerful would our faith be today if we hadn't tampered with the evidence that women are whole and created in the image of God?

Many women have carried burdens for a long time. We may have agreed to hide what is exquisite about ourselves and called it God's will. We may have stuck to the belief that we had to be obedient to male authority even when it was dangerous to our well-being. Or we may have gone through the excruciating process of leaving a community we loved because of their insistence on persecuting women. Some women may have endured punishment, shame, violence, ridicule, or banishment for believing in themselves. Women have been digging tunnels to our souls beneath the world of oppressive systems so that we might feel like human beings and inhabit ourselves. The spiritual wounds women carry within are profound. But our souls have been guiding us to wholeness and healing. Indeed, our very resurrection, our recovery, and hope lie in our ability to rise up and reclaim our lost stories.

Hidden women of the Bible have been calling out to us to

come and sit by their wild and holy fire, listen to their stories, and be healed by their sacred medicine. As we respond, we find that we were not crazy for believing that God is calling us to trust in women's leadership. A Holy One is calling our spirits to awaken and live our "one wild and precious life."[8]

When I began learning about these hidden women of the Bible, I was going through a significant transition. I had answered a call from the depths of what appeared to everyone around me to be the perfect untamed life. I was the lead singer of a popular rock band, and when I left to answer a spiritual calling, most of my friends thought I was out of my mind. I was living the rock and roll dream; I had been kissed (on the hand) by Ringo Starr, had a number one rock song on the radio, and was sharing stages with legendary rock acts of the day. I was the image of a free woman. But that's just it; it was only an image. Inside I was plagued with wounds that called out for spiritual healing. I knew I wasn't going to find it in that world. I ended up waiting tables in a downtown restaurant in Nashville to figure it out. I met a young man there who was awaiting an appointment as a United Methodist minister. When I talked with him, I felt an old, familiar tug inside of me. He was also raised in the world of Bible stories like me. He was brought up as a Nazarene and I, a Southern Baptist. We were both in church three times a week as children, immersed in Bible stories. But, in his own college and seminary experience, he had learned to read the Bible differently, from the perspective of characters who weren't traditionally portrayed as heroes. Mainly women. Through our conversations, I realized there were new stories I'd never heard before and untamed horizons in my faith journey I hadn't yet explored. I was hooked.

Three years later, we got married, and I went to seminary at Vanderbilt Divinity. In the windowless basement of the seminary library, the stories of the Bible's wild and holy women began to speak to me and lead me around the uncharted realms of the biblical world. It seemed as if they jumped off the shelves! Looking back, it feels as if they had all collectively formed some cosmic committee from the great beyond to come and rescue me, leading me on a healing journey. These books about women of the Bible were written by women who had become biblical scholars, theologians, and preachers as soon as possible back in the '50s and '60s. I knew that the United Methodist Church had been ordaining women since 1956. Still, I had not yet met the female clergy that found their voices during that time and preached, taught, and spread these stories like seeds on hardened ground. I never thought, before then, that it was a possibility for me to be ordained. But the lost stories of women in the Bible and these educated women who went after them to liberate their voices emboldened me. I had no more excuses, and I had to answer this Divine call.

As I read about these women who answered God's wild call, something awakened in me. Possibility, opportunity, and identity came through their stories. I heard the "fairytale knock at the door of the deep female psyche."[9] My creativity and imagination began to come to life in a way that didn't seem like exploitation. I imagined that I, too, could be a host to this image of God within. I began to heal as I interacted with their stories, and my own story took on a new focus and meaning rooted in the Bible.

My journey led me to become an ordained United Methodist minister. I was appointed to be a senior pastor at a church in urban Nashville. While I ministered to the community, I continued to study women's stories and write songs because music has always been that magical pathway to connecting with the sacred. I shared songs that I wrote based on their stories whenever I could sneak them into my preaching cycle. Lyrics are the perfect way to enter into women's stories. Hannah, Deborah, Elizabeth, and Mary all sang world-changing songs.

Over the last decade, as I've led workshops and shared these songs and stories with groups, I've come to understand that they bring up a lot of feelings, some of them mixed. As you read the stories, know that it's okay to be wherever you are on your journey and accept whatever feelings come up for you. As we dive into their experiences, we see that the Bible is full of imperfect people trying to understand what it means to follow God anyway. Often, our spiritual journey teaches us how to live and be at peace with our imperfection rather than striving to be perfect.

I hope this book will help you untame your own story. To free the girl you were told to be and find the person God created. To heal and discover the wholeness of God within you, to locate and name the barriers to your thriving. And a full disclaimer here, I'm not a therapist or psychologist. I'm just a pastor who has been preaching and singing these stories for a decade and found life-giving power in them. Take only what you need from this book.

I've focused on ten stories of women I call wild and holy. Each chapter begins with an original song I've written to represent the woman's voice. I've composed modern versions of their stories in the style of music that is most comfortable to me. I invite you to begin with the song. You can find a free version of the song on my website for listening at wildandholy.org, or you can download the mp3 or purchase the CD. Next, you are invited to read the biblical story that is referenced under the chapter title. I recommend one of two biblical translations, either the NRSV or Eugene Peterson's "The Message." If you don't have a copy of either of these, you can look up the passages in many different translations on www.biblegateway.com. Next, the chapter unfolds. I've shared some of my experiences inspired by these women and paired each story with an aspect of the healing journey. At the end of each chapter, I've written some questions for reflection. You can work through these alone or form a group for discussion. I have provided some space for journaling in the book. But you might want to purchase a journal or notebook to write down your thoughts.

My prayer is that this book brings you courage, strength, and hope and helps you find healing pathways. I hope my journey with these stories will inspire you to live out of your God-given gifts, wholeness, light, and beauty within.

The Song the Women Warriors Sing

The wind howls in the darkness of the longest night
The wolves cry in the distance of the wild in sight
She stands guard at the doorway of light
She carries a mirror fastened to her side
to signal a warning or prophesy
she looks into it to see Heaven's eyes

She said love needs a carriage of bronze and gold
With angels to guard it from days of old
It's been here forever we've just been told
Make a home in the cold for love

When the spirit comes it's a frightening dream
You must know the passage through the fiery ring
It's a song the women warriors sing

Maybe you've heard it in a singer's voice
Surely you've felt it in nature's course
Or known it in your heart's own choice.

CHAPTER 1

Women Warriors

(Exodus 38:8)

A woman loses her way by losing her
instinctual and wild life.
—Clarissa Pinkola Estes

I t's no surprise that the first wild and holy women of the Bible we meet appear on the iconic wilderness journey of Exodus. In the Bible's wild spaces, women cross the line between civilization and wilderness, breaking free from traditional rules and constraints. Is it really that different for us? Ever since human beings created domestic life, there has been an invisible line between the domesticated and the wild realms. When we feel trapped, wounded, and weary, the wilderness is always there on the distant horizon, calling us to cross that line and be free. We long to let the wild do its work on us. But most of us can't hang out there long enough to re-wild our souls. However, one way we can answer the call of the wild and cross that invisible line is through the enchanted world of stories.

Stories tell us who we are. They remind us that we are rooted in a wild and holy nature. Through stories that have been hidden in the wilderness regions of the biblical landscape as well as the terra firma of our world, we're discovering an ancient and liberating truth: women were warriors.

Recently, the remains of an elite Viking Warrior were discovered in Southeastern Sweden. It was previously assumed that the warrior was a man, considering the masculine lore of Viking Warriors. But the DNA of the bones confirmed a shocking truth. This elite Viking Warrior, buried in an elaborate grave with two sacrificed horses, swords, arrows, and other weaponry, was a woman.

In American history, an eyewitness account tells of a female Cherokee warrior who was found among the dead at Waya Gap during the Revolutionary War. She was "painted and striped like a warrior and armed with bows and arrows."[10] These Cherokee War Women "who distinguished themselves in battle occupied an exalted place in Cherokee political and ceremonial life."[11]

Disney's popular portrayal of "Mulan," based on an ancient Chinese song, "Ballad of Mulan," has captivated our imagination since its late 90's release. But we may have thought it was just a fairytale. Recently, "ancient remains found in the Mongolian steppe suggest that the story may have been inspired by real Xianbei women who rode horseback and probably also used bows and arrows."[12]

Female Bible scholars are unearthing similar stories in the uncharted regions of the Bible. Thanks to the work of these dedicated scholars over the past few decades, we hear stories that have been hidden in plain sight or lost in translation. Through their eyes, we're discovering the warrior women of the wilderness journey in Exodus who guarded sacred sites that housed the Holy of Holies.[13] These women warriors appear again in 1 Samuel 2:22 and yet again in the New Testament in John 18:16, guarding the entrance to the Temple where Jesus was on trial. Of course, the ultimate woman warrior, Deborah, has captivated our imagination for a while, and her accomplice, Jael. We've known about the bravery and courage of biblical women all along. But when we realize that there are untold stories in the Bible of women who were warriors, military heroes, and courageous leaders, it changes the way we see ourselves.

Just like the bones of women warriors that are beginning to tell their stories into our world, the bones of these wild and holy biblical women have new stories to tell us about old narratives. As we meet these women, something within us stirs. For those two words together, "warrior" and "woman," create "a fairytale knock at the door"[14] of the heart. If we squint across the horizon, we can imagine them standing there, guarding the entrances to the traveling sanctuary. Before there were temples, kingdoms built and lost, and before any of it was written down. Perhaps if we put our ears to the ground, we can still hear their songs.

The Wilderness Journey

The wilderness journey was epic. At first, there was no food or water, and thousands of Israelites had to rely upon God for their basic necessities. But they couldn't see God, and they had to invest in the crazy idea that they would find their way with no map. They had to trust that God would provide a guiding cloud by day and a pillar of fire by night to lead them through the wildlands. It wasn't easy, and the trauma of their past often haunted them. Images of their torture continued to play in the theater of their memory. Today, we have incredible research in the area of trauma with books such as "The Body Keeps the Score" by Bessel Van Der Kolk. We understand how trauma affects the brain and that "traumatized people become stuck, stopped in their growth because they can't integrate new experiences into their lives."[15] But in the ancient world, it took the better part of forty years for the Israelites to understand their trauma and learn how to move forward.

Even though they were geographically distant from the site of their oppression, they were still prisoners to it in their minds and couldn't forget their former lives. And although it seems counterintuitive, they longed for their past. Because even though they were slaves, at least things were predictable and familiar. They may have been tortured and oppressed, but at least they got regular food and had a place to sleep. Their inability to move on from their past, even though it was not good for them, often prevented them from investing in an unknown future. There are few things in this world more frightening than uncertainty. And yet, when God is leading us through it, this realm of the unknown can be the very place where healing and faith are born.

Their longing for the familiar was crippling at first, and it caused them to lash out at Moses and at each other. They made very little progress initially, but along the way, they began to grow as they learned to trust in a Higher Power over and against their own tragic stories. At some point along the way, they moved from being victims to becoming free people. Slowly they began to believe in their freedom and learn to rely on it as a gift from God.

Perhaps they were angry at God for letting them suffer so much, or maybe they were carrying around a lot of resentment and bitterness. But these things did not serve them well out in the wilderness. They needed to rely on something different to get through. They needed to believe in love and one another. Over time, as God gave them trials and walked with them through the hard times, they built confidence in their abilities. As their confidence and self-esteem grew, God began to bring them into a new order, from insanity to sanity. God created a new kind of stability in them as they risked learning how to move from surviving to thriving. But this took the better part of forty years. It was a long and circuitous journey.

During their journey, they came to a place where new structures were needed for their newfound faith to grow and take hold of their lives. They couldn't put new wine into old wineskins. So God gave Moses some rules for living and instructions for setting up this new community, and they began building it together. Around the time when they began to construct a sacred site for God's presence to be cared for on the earth, the women warriors appear in the story.

Love Needs a Carriage

It's likely no coincidence that our first sighting of these warrior women occurs in the wilderness. In the Bible and in our lives, the wilderness is often where we discover our greatest treasures. When we strip away our creature comforts and familiar surroundings, we often encounter something inside us that is brave, courageous, and completely unexpected. It's been there all along, a God-given gift, and perhaps we didn't realize it was there. When we peel back the layers of how we may have been taught to see the world, we begin to see it as it is, or as

God created it, natural and in harmony with creation. We learn to see things through God's eyes as we form a new perspective. Our journey into the Bible's wilderness changes us, helping us see our lives with more clarity and honesty.

When we first encounter the stories of the warrior women, we may initially be shocked. It may seem foreign to us at first. But once we begin to discover their stories, we see that they appear throughout the biblical landscape. Biblical scholar Wilda Gafney interprets these women as "prophet-warriors" (given the role of the prophet also involves a military function) and "sanctuary guardians,"[16] Given the stories of the women who acted in a military capacity such as Deborah and Jael and the women who guarded the gates mentioned previously, scholars believe that there are likely more unmentioned women who served similar roles throughout the Bible. As Gafney states: "There are an untold number of female prophets hiding in the masculine grammar and androcentric focus of the Hebrew Scriptures."[17]

Who are these "untold number" of women? This small detail that appears in Exodus 38:8 has largely escaped most of our renditions of the wilderness journey. The NRSV (New Revised Standard Version) calls them the "women who served," and these women are often referred to in other translations as the "ministering women" (American Standard Version) or the "ranks of women assigned" (Common English Bible). Gafney translates the Hebrew as "the women warriors stationed."[18]

The Israelites had been using a temporary, traveling sanctuary known as the Tent of Meeting, a site of sacred rituals. The holy tent held valuable relics that were evidence of God's presence with them on the journey. This evidence had power, too, so it had to be protected. The role of the women, some scholars surmise, was to stand at the entrances to this holy place as guardians.[19]

The traveling sanctuary was complex. A home for God's love on earth, it would house within it a sacred carriage or the Ark of the Covenant. God gave the site's dimensions to Moses and also instructions for the Ark of the Covenant. The ark would be an elaborate box, one made of acacia wood, which in some biblical traditions served as a box for the Ten Commandments, and in others, the throne of God.

This task of making a holy site to house the Ark of the Covenant on the wilderness journey involved everyone, and it was a community effort. We are told in the story that the women who guarded the entrances to the Tent of Meeting, the mobile sanctuary, even pitched in. Their bronze mirrors were used to form the washbasin that would sit outside of the inner sanctum, the Holy of Holies, where the ark would be kept. This washbasin was very special. It was the place where the priests would wash before entering the Holy of Holies. It had to be perfect.

Some scholars speculate that the mirrors were likely a part of their armor and perhaps used as signaling devices.[20] Maybe they were melted down to form the basin. Or some scholars also speculate that these women had a prophetic role, and they used their mirrors to "'divine' their prophetic visions."[21] It was not uncommon in the ancient world for mirrors to be used as prophetic devices. Exactly how the mirrors were used in service is not entirely clear. But at this moment in which the Israelites are constructing a home on earth for God's presence and love to be near, we make a new discovery. We learn that women were warrior guardians. As we come to know their stories, we see that they have many treasures to share with us. Not the least of which is their warrior woman spirit. A spirit that will come to inhabit us on our journey of healing too.

Healing Is a Journey of Circles

The journey to the Promised Land likely could have been navigated over the course of months or maybe a year or two. But the story tells us that Moses led them toward their destination for forty years. Of course, there was no such thing as Google Maps in the ancient world, and travel was very difficult. But forty years is a long time. This painful journey toward freedom must have seemed like an endless circular wandering. When we think of the wilderness journey, we often think it's a pathway *through* something, not *around* something. But as we trace their journey, it seems as if they might have been circling something. Was it their pain? Their past? Their doubt and fear? There was something at the center of their journey: a point or a place of origin. I like to think of their journey as a spiral or like the rings that make up the circumference of a tree. Each year the Israelites added another layer to their journey. They moved away from the center until, at last, they would be invited to form a new center. This new story would have hope as its origin; hope generated by the love, and the power of God to do a new thing. This new story began as they learned how to inhabit the gift of freedom.

Perhaps it took that long for them to become ready for their freedom or let go of the old stories that haunted them. They had to circle the center, which held years of trauma, oppression, and pain. They had to write new experiences over this pain enough times to build fresh pathways of courage and strength. As they became grounded in a new story, they were able to let go of the old one. Each challenge was an opportunity to build trust and courage and to believe in a new narrative. Each time they could let go a little bit, but not completely, of the pain. You see, the pain had held them together for so long that if they let go of it all at once, it might have been destabilizing. God needed to build a home in their hearts little by little; otherwise, it might have been overwhelming.

When we begin to find some freedom from the pain and wounds in our lives, it can feel destabilizing and disorienting. We may not understand what's happening. We often long for the familiar even though it wasn't good for us. Sometimes we can become trapped in a story dominated by pain and trauma, and this may be the only story we have ever known, or at least, that we can remember. When we begin to transition into our freedom, that transition can sometimes feel worse than the pain we've been carrying around in our bodies for years because it may be unfamiliar. Just as the Israelites found, even in their freedom, the challenges they faced were difficult. But they were building trust, and it took a long time for their fear to be replaced with energy for new life. God desires to bring us to a place of healing. It's not going to be easy. For some reason, our fear doesn't want to let go of us and puts up a very long, hard fight. God will lead us if we are willing and be our strength. But there are no shortcuts. If we have patience and practice being gentle with ourselves along the way, we will make it.

One day, as we stick with it, we will see that God has made a holy labyrinth out of our pain. God will build something inside you that will be stable enough to carry you into your true freedom. *Love needs a carriage of bronze and gold.* Think of the healing journey of the Israelites as God teaches you to build a sacred site in your very own heart. Healing takes time, but you can channel the spirit of the warrior woman. You can learn to guard the doorways of light in your very own heart until an altar is built and you are strong enough to carry it.

We often need to circle our pain for a while. Learning each day, each month, and each year how to move forward with our pain as our starting point. God is building something sacred in us as we do this work, and it's making us stronger. We catch a glimpse in the mirrors of our lives, in the faces of those who have come with us on this journey, and in the image of our own reflection as we learn to love ourselves. We catch glimpses of what our lives can be here and there, on the horizon, darting across. We share these glimpses of our healing with our companions on the journey. They become real. We let go of those who have brought us harm. Notice on the Israelite journey, they are never allowed to go back but only forward. Though they may regress in their minds, they have to work it out and find solutions, or their regression could become lethal to their progress.

Eventually, God helps us to create order out of disorder, sanity out of insanity, stability out of instability, uncovering the lost stories hidden inside of us. The warrior women appear from nowhere, standing guard at the doorways of light: teaching us their sacred songs, the songs that bring heaven to earth, distilling the fear on the horizon and giving us Divine courage and strength.

Reflection

1. If you were to make a map of your own healing journey where would you find yourself? Circle the point on the map provided to find the center point for your healing journey. Use this guide to determine where you are presently.

   a. Still in a difficult situation that is harmful to you?

   b. Feeling trapped?

   c. Feeling disoriented or lost?

   d. I've already escaped a harmful situation and I'm on the pathway to my healing.

   e. I'm in the middle of a healing journey but I'm a little lost.

   f. I'm in the wilderness and I've got a good plan, but I need some resources to go further.

   g. I've just about made it out of the wilderness and I'm ready to find out what's next. How do I inhabit my God-given freedom?

   h. I'm on the other side of that wilderness journey and now I want to dig into what my future looks like. I have something to share with others.

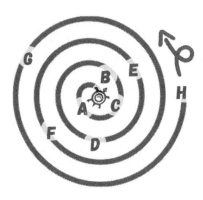

2. Now that you have an idea of where your center point is, let's have some fun with channeling the archetype of the woman warrior. As you scan the horizon of where you are, what do you see around you? Are there obstacles or challenges? Are there threats? What is your mission? In what direction are you headed? Where do you feel God is calling you to go? Use the space provided to write down some answers.

3. Share your inventory with others in your discussion group or with a trusted and encouraging friend. Make it real.

4. In the next space, write down where you feel you are headed in this phase of your journey. Where would you like to be?

5. Make this point on the horizon a goal, write out your goal in your journal. Explore the following questions: What is my mission and what is standing in the way? Where am I feeling led to go? What is my goal?

JOURNAL SPACE

The Stars Fought from Heaven

It's not mine anymore
I gave it to the wind
"Awake," it cried, "awake"
and sing again
Well, here it is
Your life is poetry
And every time you love
You set the hurt of the world free
You set the hurt of the world free (for you)

The stars fought from heaven
But my heart was with the ones
who fought without weapons
Without weapons they came
Knowing love would reign

A war, a God, a people
Coming undone
Even with war in the air
A beautiful poem is spun
There's a curse on everyone
But we can break free
I saw it in their eyes
The ones who came believing
The ones who came believing (for them)

CHAPTER 2

Deborah:
Woman of Fire

(Judges 4, 5)

Don't be afraid, child,
the stories are always there.
–Mary E. Pearson

The first time I saw a female hero who felt true to form in a blockbuster movie, I remember feeling something inside me awaken. It was a new feeling, and it was strange. I watched a gritty Charlize Theron in the film "Mad Max: Fury Road" play a role as the character Imperator Furiosa, who liberated other women. Of course, it was just a movie, but seeing a woman larger than life, grungy, and bold, helped me to believe in myself in new ways. She was, like Deborah, a woman of fire.

It's been challenging for most of my life to own the power within me as a woman—the power of creation, strength, and profound wisdom. It's a unique combination that we carry within us, the ability to be vulnerable and courageous at the same time. It feels like this power has mostly been in service to someone else or to a system that kept it tame. But now I understand that we all have this fire within us, a God-given gift; it's the image of God within. This image takes its particular form in each of our unique personalities. It comes with the package of being human, created in the image of God. I know that there have been many times when I've felt that I had to disguise this fiery spirit or hide it to be acceptable. I also know that it has been hard to access, covered over by wounds, pierced by insults, and bullied by shame and labeling. But it is still there, a seed that won't die and insists on living. It burst open a little bit more when I witnessed Furiosa liberating the oppressed in an apocalyptic world.

We often hear that the Bible teaches us that women are the inferior gender and are to be subservient to men, the superior gender. There are also the very odd teachings in both the Old and New Testaments ranging from how women should dress to what they are required to do if their virgin bodies are violated before marriage - marry the man who violated her! (Deuteronomy 22:28,29). I understand that these teachings still undergird oppressive practices that women are forced to endure on this side of my healing journey. In some cultures, "biblical" perspectives of women are used to condone practices such as genital mutilation and the prostitution of daughters.

These long-held cultural views of women as the "inferior" gender have led to much human suffering for girls and women. So, we often experience Bible shock when we read stories of women who were liberators and leaders of their communities.

We may not have thought such women existed in the Bible. We've been told for so long that God created women as secondary beings. So we often have a difficult time believing these stories at first. I even had a parishioner who found these stories offensive. But it's true; there are a few Imperator Furiosas in the Bible too. We just have to look a little bit harder to find them.

In the book of Judges chapters four and five, we find two such women, Deborah and Jael. They are liberators in a book that resembles the apocalyptic nightmare of the "Mad Max" series of movies. At the beginning of Judges, we meet Deborah, a military leader and a judge, who led a rebellion against the Canaanites who were oppressing the Israelites. Her partner, Jael, killed Sisera, the Canaanite army leader, and was granted victory for the battle. Two women led a rebellion, and the people of God had peace for forty years. This story is not exactly a familiar one, but it's a powerful narrative for women worldwide.

However, as we walk more deeply into the book of Judges, things become dangerous for women. We find stories of women who were raped (the Levite's concubine), sacrificed (Jephthah's daughter), rounded up by force, and abducted (the virgins of Judges 21). The book of Judges evolves into dark and gruesome stories of people gone astray. Women pay the price: they become victims of violence in a society that no longer values them. It has been said that a culture can be judged by the way in which it treats women. In Judges, we often see a mirror of our own experience, our lives may begin in promising ways, but as we grow into womanhood, we often wake up to how women are still being oppressed in the world. With such a high rate of violence against women in our world, we may wonder when, if ever, oppression will come to an end. These stories help us navigate through the challenges we face in our world.

A Woman Leads Them

Deborah is a great Mother of Israel who hovers over a violent book, giving us hope. In Judges chapters 4 and 5, we discover that she was a prophet, judge, and military leader when her people, the Israelites, were oppressed by the Canaanites. She sat at her palm tree and judged the people's disputes. Her word was the law in a time when there were no kings, only judges appointed by God. Her name means "bee" or "wasp." Indeed, her actions have quite the sting, and I often think of her as a queen bee. The story tells us that she was the "wife of Lappidoth." Some scholars interpret "Lappidoth" not as an actual man but as a "torch" or "lightning."[22] Deborah is known as a woman wedded to fire or woman of torches, as she calls her people to rise up out of oppression.

In Judges, we learn that the people were reckless and did as they pleased, but Deborah's role was to bring order to the chaos as a judge and prophet. People came to her with their disputes. She was the one who decided what was fair. At the time, she was the highest authority in her community. Even so, many of her people thought she was out of her mind when she called upon them to fight an impossible battle. The Canaanites had nine hundred chariots of iron, a powerful army, and an arsenal of the latest weaponry. And what did the Israelites have to defend themselves? Not much. They were poor and scattered. Maybe they could have collected a few spears, some arrows, and a few shields among them.

So when Deborah called the tribes of Israel to come

and fight, to rebel against their oppressors and reclaim their God-given freedom, many refused to come. But some did. The ones who came and followed her into battle were praised for their faithful response. What happened to the ones who didn't? Well, she put a curse on them. Yes, she was that powerful!

Just as Deborah sang, God caused the rains to come and flood out the Canaanites' chariots; they were stuck in the mud and useless. God even caused the stars to fight from heaven that day, the story tells us. Deborah's victory was secure, and we read that they had peace in the land for forty years. Deborah was a hero, but we don't often hear about her bravery, leadership skills, and ability to get her people to follow her into an impossible battle. What a powerful woman appointed by God at a critical time in the lives of God's people.

Deborah was in the fight of her life. It was a fight, not only for the freedom of her people but also for the story of female leadership in the ancient world to be told and not undermined through revisionist history. The narrators left her story in the book of Judges. But have we really heard it yet?

Awake and Sing

Deborah answers the call to "awake and sing." A Divine call to awaken to the moment at hand, the moment of freedom; to sing a prophecy of battle, a battle cry for her people's well-being. A daunting, impossible task. But we are to understand that God has prepared her for this task; she likely already possessed the skills to lead a military rebellion against a formidable army. God had already given her what she needed to accomplish her mission. Still, she had to say "yes" and follow that awakening without turning back. She did not go alone.

Barak, another military leader, went with her. He even told her that he wouldn't attempt such an impossible feat if she weren't with him. It may have been her idea, and the people may have followed her call, but she also had to be present for the actual event. Otherwise, the people might have lost hope. In Deborah, we find a leader who risked trusting her God given intuition and used it to lead her people to freedom.

We often have intuitive feelings within ourselves. Intuition is an internal, God-given navigation device that we use to find our way in the world. But so often, women are taught to doubt our intuition, to be suspicious of our voices. We are often taught from a very young age to be obedient to male authority. That the big decisions in our lives need to be rubber-stamped by male permission to be considered "legitimate." We often second guess our internal guidance because we have been conditioned not to trust ourselves first. Many women find it difficult to trust an inner voice. The voices that have taught us what we are supposed to be are often so much louder than the still small voice within, the one that leads us to the version of ourselves that God has created. But in time, we can learn to trust this inner voice as we ask God to lift the barriers to our thriving.

Freedom from Oppression

The word "oppression" has many levels of meaning. It can be physical, but it can also be emotional or spiritual, meaning to burden, put down, or ridicule. In American culture, it might mean that a woman is discriminated against due to gender or race. Perhaps she is held back, overlooked, or not paid equally for the same work as men. It could mean that a woman is expected to endure sexual harassment to keep her job. Domestic violence, rape, bullying, and shaming are all forms of oppression. In some countries: the laws fail to represent women's rights as human beings. In some parts of the world, women are not as free as men in the public sphere. Of course, it wasn't until the last century that women's rights in America began to shift, such as gaining the right to vote, for example (1920). Even for women in United States, some freedoms are still relatively recent in the span of human existence.

As women gain more freedom, we are supposed to become less oppressed. That's the idea, anyway. But as we are finding, just because laws shift and women move forward, sometimes the mental oppression remains and can be paralyzing. The pain, loss, and wounds are still present and need healing. We may be physically free but still be enslaved in our minds and souls. Recent research tells us that the body remembers traumatic experiences, and it even stores these memories in our brains and bodies.[23] We often need specialized trauma therapy in order to feel and live in the freedom available to us today. Because "trauma need not be a life sentence,"[24] healing is possible.

Sometimes it's even difficult to put a name to our own pain, loss, and wounds. Sometimes the pain is stored in memories we have carried around for so long; they make up a heaviness within that we are accustomed to carrying that feels oppressive. This weight may have become so familiar that we may not even know who we are without the heavy memories of loss and pain. Bible stories can really help us to unburden ourselves and begin to let go of the pain. Because as we hear stories of women who have transcended the bounds of oppression with God's help, we feel something within us become a little bit lighter. As we interact with them, it often becomes easier for us to find words for our own pain. As we find words for our pain and name what happened to us, the pain begins to lose its power over us. The stories of the untamed women of the Bible enable us to catch little glimpses of our freedom on the horizon as we respond to God's wild belief in us.

The stories are critical to our healing process. When we read the book of Judges and experience the stories of violence against women as well as the stories of powerful women standing up to violence, it stirs something within us and gives us the courage to face the mass of pain within and begin to dismantle it slowly. We begin to thaw out on the inside; feelings that were once frozen begin to melt slowly. We do this as we tell stories of what happened to women in the Bible alongside the stories of what happened to us too. It not only dismantles the pain but it helps us to see that there is a better future waiting for us. The stories become our healing companions.

When we experience Deborah's story, we learn to see things differently. Having her as a hero awakens a spirit inside of us, our inner "woman of fire" begins to live. She gives us the courage to trust our inner voice, to develop it, and to follow it. As we do, we see that there is a pathway out of oppression, and we can help others as we trust our own journey. It won't be easy, but over time new stories will be written from our lives and our struggles in the world. We will learn how to share these stories with other women who will believe us. This process of sharing lost stories will produce handholds for other women to rise up out of pain and loss. Knowing that in Deborah's story, God's people followed a female leader, a liberator, an imperator, and a warrior into battle leads us to consider what other stories we have been missing. What has been lost inside of us? And what might we find if we walk a little while with Deborah? What would she say to those of us who are afraid of following the voice deep inside? God is calling all of us to trust a woman's voice.

Reflection

1. Name one thing that Deborah's story stirs inside of you. For example, a gift inside of you that you feel God has given you or a unique expression of who you are.

2. Name a few things that you feel prevent you from using this gift. It could be shame, feeling vulnerable, discouragement, threats, or lack of experience. Use the journal space provided to put words to what you're feeling.

3. What do you feel would give you greater access to this gift? People who believe in you? Education? Training? Ask God to show you the barriers.

4. What evidence can you create that would help you see this gift coming to life? For example, a poet writes more poetry and shares it. An author creates an idea for a book and finds the support she needs to create it. A musician gets training in her instrument and finds others to rehearse with and perform. What can you create that would show that you are serious about this gift?

Journal Space

Steady My Prey

Come hide away, my brother.
Come drink and rest your weary head,
lie down in my bed.
Ten thousand men coming for you,
and all your army is dead
to a woman you have fled. (repeat)

Should I lift my wings to dance and sing?
Should I spread my wings
and let you have your way?
No I will lift my wings, to feign sheltering
While I steady my prey,
While I steady...

One hand to the hammer,
One hand to the iron stake.
No protest did you raise
Your mother waits at her window.
She's worried for your delay.
Two women for every man her friends will say.
Two women for every man, hey....

CHAPTER 3

Jael:
the Slayer

(Judges 4, 5)

The cave you fear to enter
holds the treasure you seek.
–Joseph Campbell

"Tell me, what is it you plan to do with your one wild and precious life?"[25] It's often tough to give ourselves permission to pursue a "wild and precious life." Perhaps we've been convinced that we are not worthy of investing in ourselves, or our fear of failure has paralyzed us. Maybe we are just struggling to survive, and following something as elusive as a wild and precious life seems like a luxury we can't afford. That doesn't change the fact that it's there, our one wild and precious life, waiting to be ignited.

Martin Buber said, "Every person born into this world represents something new, something that never existed before, something original and unique."[26] It is up to every person to develop this unique quality. There's a pathway that connects us to the place where this exceptional, God-given quality resides. It often reveals itself through something we love doing or something that we do naturally out of our gifts and talents. The goal is to learn how to access this place that is our natural creativity, where our inspiration lives. From this center we construct a self that lives more closely to our True Nature, a gift of God to every human being. We are all created in God's image, and each one of us expresses this image in unique ways.

The poet Rumi said, "Let yourself be silently drawn by what it is you truly love."[27] People who are fortunate enough to work at what they truly love are blessed to unite their vocation and the pathway of self-discovery. But as women, we are often discouraged from exploring this idea of what we truly love. We are often even afraid to ask the question. We may feel unequipped or lack the support systems we need to respond faithfully. Perhaps it never occurred to us that choosing was even an option.

Of course, we love our children, families, and friends. But there is often something deeper than these loves, which is a well of living water that supplies all the other loves. We may not have felt as if we've been granted access to this well of living water; we may have thought that others prevented us from reaching it. As Jesus said to the Samaritan woman at the well, "if (only) you knew the gift." We may feel cut off from access to our God-given gifts. Still, they are there, waiting to be drawn from our inner resources.

We see this struggle playing out with women's stories in the Bible too. Women are often portrayed as "secondary characters in a male drama."[28] The legal situation for a woman in the Old Testament was quite different from modern society. Alice Ogden Bellis, in her book, *Helpmates, Harlots and Heroes: Women's Stories in the Hebrew Bible,* describes a woman's legal status in the Old Testament as a "non-person . . . usually an inferior in a male-centered, male-dominated society."[29] We may relate to feeling like a "non-person" when we feel cut off from expressing ourselves in a manner that feels authentic to who we are. So, when we come across Jael's story, there is something in it that moves us deeply as she strikes out against her oppressor. It stirs a little mini awakening inside us when we experience a woman under these conditions acting out of a sense of agency, becoming a female hero, something she wasn't supposed to be. Jael becomes an actor rather than a reactor, the main character in the story. In a book in which women are preyed upon, Jael becomes the hunter. She flips the script, turning the target on her back into a weapon.

Most Blessed of Women

Jael is known as the woman who received the glory of the battle Deborah waged. Deborah even prophesied in advance that a woman would be the hero. Jael's story is narrated in Judges 4 and appears in Deborah's prophetic song in Judges 5. She slew the leader of the Canaanite army, Sisera, and drove a tent stake through his head. This is the lore of the old, old story that most of us have never heard. But behind the lore lives another dimension: a hidden story of how Jael came to understand that her very own soul was a thing worth protecting in a world that told her otherwise.

Some scholars speculate that Jael may have been a member of a harem. The truth is we really don't know. She was a part of an independent tribe known as the Kenites. The Kenites did not affiliate with the Canaanites or the Hebrews, but they had diplomatic relationships with both. They were known as blacksmiths and worked with the forged metal of the age. The story tells us about the nine hundred chariots of iron that belonged to the Canaanite army, but the text itself seems to be set in the Bronze Age. Perhaps the story was told as the ages overlapped; we're not really sure. At any rate, Jael's tribe likely did business with the Canaanites as the region occupied by the Kenites was probably neutral territory.

After the Canaanite army was defeated by Deborah and her army, only the Canaanite army leader, Sisera, survived. He took off on the run; he knew Deborah was out for him. He sought refuge in Jael's tent, perhaps thinking it was a safe space. We are not directly told in the story that raping and pillaging was a common practice of the victors. But Sisera's mother's maids insinuate it as they seek to comfort her, saying, "Are they (the men) not finding and dividing the spoil? A girl or two for every man" (Judges 5:30). It's not clear if that's what Sisera had in mind when he sought refuge in Jael's tent.

Jael gave Sisera something to drink and told him to rest. And without hesitating, as he slept, she took the tools of her trade, which included a hammer and a tent peg, and drove it through his temple. The story tells us that "he sank, he fell, he lay still at her feet; at her feet he sank, he fell, where he sank, there he lay dead" (Judges 5:27). In this great flipping of the script, it is not the women who become the spoils of war but Sisera himself. The anticipated hero of the story, Sisera, becomes the victim, and the anticipated victim becomes the hero. For her bravery, Jael is given the title "Most Blessed of Women."

We might not understand such a gory display of violence or why it seems glorified in this story. But if we focus only on a literal interpretation, we will lose our way in the story. When we learn to read Bible stories, we need to play by the rules of the story, which are metaphor, symbolism, intrigue, character development, conflict, plot, and the storyteller's mystique, among other things. We need to remember that we are walking through a story, and the storyteller's audience would be searching for what the story is portraying rather than focusing only on factual details. Some layers of fact and history may be included in the story. But meaning often comes to us through the medium of the story, and in this case, through a female hero's voice and actions.

One of the many tools biblical storytellers use is symbolism. We can often look at symbols in the stories to find meaning. Sisera is entering Jael's tent, her inner sanctum, her home, and her intimate space. What does this space represent? It is symbolic of her very self. But something spectacular and rare unfolds in her inner sanctum. We see that she is given the power to not only become a hero of war but also to protect herself. She realizes that she is a person who is worth saving, and she doesn't rely on anyone else to do it. She saves herself instead. Furthermore, the man who has developed a reputation for taking women as spoils of war now perishes at the hands of a woman he finally could not violate.

All the gory slashing aside, it is a story of two women who were victorious and triumphant in a major battle in a world in which they were supposed to become only the "spoils of war." They took agency upon themselves to not just become the equal of men but to live into their fullest potential as women. Deborah and Jael won an impossible battle by rising up of their own volition. Men readily followed these two women into the battlefield, where they prevailed victoriously.

Protecting What You Truly Love

Jael's story shows us that we all have a right to protect what God has given to us. An identity, interior life, and an inner sanctum that is worth exploring. In fact, as Martin Buber said, it is our calling to do so! God has already made way for us to follow the pathway.

We all have an inner warrior woman: an inner Jael who won't let anyone steal from our sacred warehouse anymore. Our wholeness is worth finding. We may need to meet the demands of a job and a family, but there is still time and space that we can set aside and explore. It begins with the question, "What it is that I truly love?" You may have to ask this question a hundred times before you find an answer that fits. That's okay. Just keep asking. There will come a time when you are tired and weary of dancing for others while your inner life starves. And when that time comes, you will know what to do. You have met your inner Jael, and you are capable of nurturing and protecting the vulnerable life inside of you waiting to be born. God is at your side.

Reflection

1. Can you recall one of your earliest memories as a child in which you were happy doing something you loved? Can you remember what it was? What did you love about it?

2. Can you connect this memory with something you have done as an adult or teenager that gave you the same feeling of being connected to what you truly loved?

3. Name an activity that really inspires you or something that makes you feel connected to creativity, to God, and to love. Does this activity connect to something you did as a child?

4. Now ask the question, "What is it that I truly love?" Jot down some answers in the journal space.

Journal Space

Seen Through

Somebody hid your love away
Buried in an unmarked grave,
And all your life you suspected
It would be resurrected someday.
She makes you feel different,
Like a man whose done the right thing.
And in her words you can finally hear
The song of your heart sing.

So, what if the world ends tomorrow?
She's got a light on you.
Feels so good to be seen by someone
Seen through.

Nobody plays by the rules
In the politics of justice.
You got battered by the waves
Your vessel near corrupted,
But it will all wither away...
All those deals that you made
For a better world.
Now you've only yourself to save.

In the halls of the great reformers
Purging the sins of your fathers,
Putting a price on religion
Forgetting, forgetting
Love, love is free.

CHAPTER 4

Huldah:
the Seer

(2 Kings 22; 2 Chronicles 34)

*There is no greater agony than bearing
an untold story inside you.*
—Maya Angelou

The search for hidden treasure has always captured our imagination. There are numerous shows, movies, and books on the subject. Some people spend their entire lives searching for buried treasure. Wealth beyond imagination is allegedly hiding in the secret places of our world. But what about the treasure that each of us is carrying within? Are we doomed to spend our lives searching outside of ourselves to find value? All the while, an inner storehouse of wealth awaits to be discovered, explored, and shared.

Jesus said that we would find our greatest treasures within, a realm he referred to as the kingdom of heaven or the kingdom of God. A place that doesn't require a treasure map to find. He told us that a sacred treasure is alive in each of us, in our hearts (Luke 17:21). He seemed to believe that what is within has much more value than whatever gold or silver we might chase here on earth. But it's a strange idea to us in the modern age. What exactly is this elusive kingdom of heaven within? Does it live alongside all of those other terrible things inside of us that we can't seem to control, like fear and anxiety? How do we access it? Perhaps his statements about what the kingdom of heaven is like can help us understand its hidden nature and why the journey to it is so vital to our development.

Jesus speaks about the kingdom of heaven or the kingdom of God within us all in the Gospel of Matthew. People were intrigued about it, so they frequently asked him to describe it. He used simile, comparing it to things that would have been very familiar to a first-century audience. He spoke of this sacred realm as a treasure hidden in a field and the most refined pearl that ends the jewelry merchant's quest for perfection. He said that it is like a tiny mustard seed that grows in the earth and produces a beautiful tree in which the birds of the air might nest. He also referred to it as the yeast hidden in the bread that causes nourishment to rise. He was getting at something we all seem to have trouble seeing at times: God's love within us all. We may find it impossible to believe that God would invest something valuable within each of us. Or we might be bitter with so much anger and hurt that we see it as a cruel joke that God has placed something within us yet dangles it in front of us like a carrot on a stick we can never quite grasp. But the truth is, God never intended for us to live our lives like dogs chasing their tails. This is the grand illusion of pain and oppression. As we work through our pain and embrace the healing process, we begin to discover our treasure, and our arduous quest gives way to newfound freedom. "We all have something to offer the world, but we have to put forth the effort to claim it."[30]

We gain strength as we learn to trust God's love in our dark night of the soul. We learn to see in the dark what lies hidden, the treasures of our very own souls. But we often need others to help us find it: those who see in us what we can't see in ourselves. Perhaps you have had a friend, grandmother, or a special someone in your life who saw something unique in you and wasn't afraid to encourage you.

It was the job of prophets in the Old Testament to see hidden treasures in the hearts of humankind. It was a Divine way of seeing with the ability to turn human hearts, bent on greed and power and mired in anxiety and fear, back to God's love. They became an invisible bridge to the kingdom of heaven during some very dark times on earth.

Prophets had a wide array of duties in the ancient Israelite world. From interpreting Divine oracles to recruiting disciples, appointing monarchs, military leadership, singing songs, gathering the community, and more. Their voice acted as an oral, spiritual navigation device before sacred words were written down to guide humanity.

Huldah was a prophet who is mentioned in 2 Kings 22:14–20 and 2 Chronicles 34:22–28, a seer. She likely taught in matters of holy law at the temple gates. She had the gift of seeing hidden things in the hearts of people. She must have made a lasting impression because there are gates at the temple mount known as The Huldah Gates even to this day. Huldah specializes in helping us on this quest to find what God has hidden in our hearts, too.

Learning to See in the Dark

By the time we meet the prophet Huldah, late 7th Century BCE, the northern kingdom of Israel had been conquered. The two kingdoms had been in conflict, at peace, and all states in between. In Huldah's day, the Temple had been established for some time in Jerusalem. Huldah was a part of the royal court in Judah's southern kingdom, and her husband, Shallum, was in charge of the king's wardrobe. From her story told in 2 Kings 22:14–20 and 2 Chronicles 34:22–28, we learn that she resided in the Second Quarter in Jerusalem, which was an area of the Temple Mount's massive expanse.

Huldah enters the story at a critical time. King Josiah had been undertaking a massive cleanup project that meant removing all of the idols from the sacred sites and establishing his orthodox version of faith. His father and grandfather, also kings, in his view and the view of the biblical narrators, had just about destroyed everything sacred to the Israelites. Holy relics had been lost or were being defiled. One day Josiah's workers found a lost sacred scroll hidden inside the Temple walls and brought it to him. The scroll or the "writing of the Teaching"[31] may have contained portions of Deuteronomy. We are told that when Josiah examined it, he was terrified and overcome with grief. He realized this was likely a missing piece to the giant puzzle of restoration. He knew he needed a prophet to interpret it.

He could have taken it to Jeremiah, a popular prophet, a contemporary of Huldah. But instead, he sent a delegation to the prophet Huldah to inquire about these scrolls. She told them what the lost scroll had to say. She authenticated it as God's Word and warned them that it meant destruction, an end of one world, and the beginning of something new. But people would suffer, and buildings would fall. She told him that this was because the people had turned their backs on God, love, mercy, grace, and kindness. Instead, they had preferred to devote themselves to the gods they could manipulate. God was always clear: his love was free. And he didn't want things like gold or silver. His love couldn't be bought, sold, or used to control others. Because what were once sacred practices had become so corrupted in the hearts of the people and the Temple, God was going to do a restart. Huldah was the one to proclaim it and send the news of God's Word to the king. Some thirty years later, the Temple was destroyed, and many Israelites were taken into captivity. She was spot on, but it took a long time for her words to ring true. She called people back to the place where they could love God with all their hearts, mind, and soul.

Josiah was moving forward on a hunch. God had planted a seed of wholeness inside of him, and he wasn't going to rest until he restored his kingdom to this vision. Even though he carried God's vision within his heart, some of the pathways to bringing it to fruition had become overgrown. He lived in a time when sacred practices had become distorted by greed, dishonest intentions, and corrupt power. It was an agonizing road for Josiah as his heart longed to see God's wholeness come to life. When the lost scroll was discovered, unburied from the sacred site, and brought to his attention, it resurrected something within him. Love itself, a holy, Divine treasure. It struck a sacred chord within him, and he knew it was God's doing.

But instead of rejoicing, he was deeply grieved. He ripped his clothes and went into a dark night of the soul. He accepted guidance from a woman, Huldah, the only one who could deliver the truth and was not blinded by power, greed, or ambition. She was a sacred seer. She saw Josiah, saw through him, and led him to the light. What's even more astounding is that she was the first person in the biblical text to authenticate written words as the Word of God.

Often when we begin our healing journey and find hidden stories, feelings, and memories inside us, we also feel sad, troubled, and angry. We are touching a process of grief that we have never allowed ourselves to enter before. We have been busy keeping up the business of our lives of survival. We are often just moving forward like zombies in a blind haze. This usually means we have been pleasing others, gaining approval, appeasing authority figures, keeping everyone calm, becoming successful, failing miserably, and avoiding conflict. Or we are hiding or running, fighting or fleeing. Until we begin the healing journey, we realize that these are the behaviors we have used to stay alive and survive. Once we locate a hidden person underneath the weight of all this chaos, we see that she has been there all along—our God-given inner wisdom.

Our hidden inner wisdom has been with us all this time, speaking to us and telling us that some things, the false things, can finally come to a slow end. Over time the walls that have been built up around our hearts will crumble. The things that have kept us from accessing our gifts within us will slowly disappear. These survival behaviors will let go of us gradually as we become aligned with God's love and wholeness that has been locked inside of us all this time, waiting to be discovered.

Reformation of the Heart

It's difficult for us to comprehend what it was like to experience God during Huldah's time. Religion and politics were like two sides of the same coin; they weren't separated as we think of them today. It might be one of the reasons why we have such a hard time separating the system of patriarchy from God's Word. Since a patriarchal system was preferred as the way to organize society, we tend to read Bible stories from that perspective. But "the Bible didn't invent patriarchy."[32] It had been around a long time.

When we encounter stories of women who are doing God's work outside the bounds of a patriarchal system like the prophets Huldah, Deborah, and the women warriors, it gives us a sense that God's love is boundless. We understand that though these were traditionally assumed to be "male-only" jobs, God recruited a woman to do them when she was suited for the role. As scholars have revealed, there were multiple female prophets in biblical Israel.[33] In Isaiah 8:3, there is the female prophet with whom Isaiah conceived a child. There are the female prophets, plural, of Israel that Ezekiel condemns in 13:15–17. There is also Noadiah, a mighty Israelite female prophet, who opposes Nehemiah in 6:14.

Even though we generally assume the Bible was written from a patriarchal perspective, we see that the narrators left these stories of powerful female prophets in the Bible. What are they telling us? Often what is hidden holds the key to our growth. The hidden stories of women of the Bible contain the key for us to find the hidden stories in ourselves. These are the ones waiting for us to have the courage to go looking for them and speak them into the world.

Sometimes it takes a disruptive event for us to see through the chaos in our lives. We've been trying to create order out of chaos for so long that we just haven't had time to pay attention. But when we slow down and do the intentional work of healing, we make conscious contact with God's gentle power in our lives. God begins to see through us and calls forth the image of God already within us all. We become restless, sad, and angry, but all of these emotions bring us out of our sealed cocoon and rock-hard denial. We learn that it's okay to feel. Our feelings and emotions lead us to something greater than ourselves. But at this critical juncture, when we can feel as if there is no guiding force, we need our inner prophet, our inner Huldah, to help us see. We need her to help us find our inner voice of wisdom to lead us down the healing pathway. She is a seer that can help us find our way in the darkness of our struggles.

Just as Josiah had to tear down some walls to uncover the hidden Word of God, we also need to allow our healing process to tear down some of the layers of hurt and pain that have been insulating us from our feelings. Our feelings lead us to God. When we can interpret our feelings and express them in a safe group of empathetic listeners, we are seen and heard; we open the locked doorway to the treasure within ourselves. We worry less about the doom and angst in the world, and we begin to see beauty, hope, and even joy growing inside of us. There is still pain, grief, and loss. But alongside these blooms, something new—hope. This hope guides us even in our darkest days. Our pain no longer traps us: there is a light within that calls out to us. We are on the right path. It feels good to be seen, seen through.

Reflection

1. What are some of the walls that you feel have been built up around your "inner knowing" or your heart? Who built these walls?

2. God has planted a vision in all of us and in each of our hearts. This vision is a part of who we are and who God has created us to be. It's usually connected to some kind of mission and the things that we feel we were put here to do in this lifetime. We all have a sense of what this is, but sometimes it gets hidden from us by trauma, wounds, or pain. But the goal is to transform the pain and trauma into healing and often, this helps us to focus on a mission. With God's help, we do this slowly. Some first steps are beginning to learn how to see through the walls of pain to your heart. Become a seer. Here are some exercises to get you started on channeling your inner Huldah.

Exercises

1. Prayer. Prayer is a wonderful tool. It gets us in touch with the great Seer, God, the Divine, the Creator, the Higher Power. Take some time to slow down; learn to breathe deeply and develop a prayer life that is rooted in your healing.

2. Become your own companion. What are you passionate about? What did you dream about doing as a young girl? If you could have one mission in this life what would it be? Begin writing a mission statement. There are lots of free resources online to help you craft one.

3. Do one thing each week. What is one thing you can do each week to help develop this mission?

4. Still confused about your mission? Try out this quote by Frederich Beuchner: "The place God calls you to is the place where your deep gladness and the world's deep hunger coincide."[34] Just try to name your "deep gladness" and find out where it fits into the world's "deep hunger." Take your time and go slowly.

Journal Space

Too Late to Be Free

All I wanted in this lost, lonely world
Was a mother or a father to claim.
So when the soldiers came
for the last of the pure girls,
I had nothing left to lose, I had everything to gain.
One by one the men paraded us before the king:
I did just as I was told, I performed to please.
Even though I hid my true identity,
He fell in love with an orphan girl and made her the
queen.

It's too late to be free,
It happened so fast.
The hand of destiny is a strange thing;
It's too late to be free.
I have the power to save everyone,
Everyone but me.

Once it's written down, oh, who will ever see
Through the cracks in the mortar of the monarchy?
Who will hear the cries
of the banished ones before me?
Trapped behind the iron clad walls
of a story we can believe.

I don't want your pity,
I'm done with the masquerade.
You'd rather make me a martyr
Than to get the story straight.
Don't wait 'till it's. . .

CHAPTER 5

Esther:
The Survivor

(Book of Esther)

What would happen if one woman told the
truth about her life?
The world would split open.
—Muriel Rukeyser

When I was a little girl, I would make up fantastical tales about events and share them with my grandmother. Looking down at me with her hands on her hips, she would smile, and in a playful voice, ask, "Are you telling me a story?" What she meant was, are you telling me what really happened, or the fairytale version?

We tell stories all the time. It's how we make meaning out of the inexplicable. We use stories to keep fear and anxiety from overwhelming us. Ever notice that when you've finished reading a great novel or viewed an excellent movie, you often feel better and more hopeful about life? Or maybe an issue you were trying to resolve takes on new meaning. Stories give us perspective on the world; they speak to us at the soul level, where our deepest wounds and greatest potential live side by side. Stories help us turn our fear into energy. They are agents of transformation.

Fairytales are some of the oldest known stories of our time. More aged, even than some of the texts of the Bible. Scholars have speculated that some fairytales might be as ancient as 6,000 years old. The fairy or folk tale genre has been around a very long time, helping humanity make meaning out of what can often seem meaningless. Joseph Campbell, an author whom George Lucas cited as being inspirational for the creation of the "Star Wars" series, has written volumes about myth-making throughout history. He explains that the act of creating myths (or stories) has often been an attempt to chase away that deep level of anxiety all of us carry around about the unknown.[35] It seems that if we can tell a story about our fear and anxiety, we can work through it. Stories are quite magical that way, soothing us with words.

But even though fairytales are lovely and magical and help us make meaning, there are often many details left out of our ancient, mythical stories. When we hear "Little Red Riding Hood," for example, we are so focused on how we can relate to her that we forget the troubling details absent from the story. We become immersed in the scene as she walks through a dark forest filled with unseen predators; we relate to her when her good deeds get her into trouble. We see our powerlessness in her fragility and all of the outside players that act upon her. As we experience the obstacles she faces in the story, we see challenges and solutions in our lives that may have been previously hidden. Stories unlock a passageway inside of us to the soul's ancient wisdom. But we often become so engrossed in the fairytale nature of stories that we overlook missing details. Such as, why is a little girl walking alone through a dangerous forest filled with rabid wolves? Why was she abandoned by whoever was supposed to be watching her? And why does her frail grandmother live so far out in the woods alone without anyone to take care of her?

These odd details don't seem necessary to conveying the actual meaning of the fairytale. When we consider them, it seems to take the magic out of the story. That's the problem with fairytales; they give us an enchanted version of real life rather than a factual retelling of accounts.

Esther

The story of Esther feels like a fairytale. A young, beautiful orphan wins a contest for the king's favor and ends up becoming a queen. A lost, poor, and disenfranchised girl finds her prince, and the rest of the story is a tale of enchantment. The bad guys lose, the good guys win. All is well in the kingdom; the castle is safe. It's a story we want to believe because it's the Cinderella version. But it's not the whole story of the book of Esther found in the Bible.

The actual version has jagged teeth and loss and shows how trapped Esther remained even as the queen of a powerful domain. We often see Esther as a hero because she risked her life to save her people, and of course, she was. But when we dig deeper into the story, we can see that even as a hero, Esther was a victim. She was doomed to appease a fickle king—a king who developed a reputation for banishing his queen. To deny the king's summoning meant termination. To appear before him without his summoning meant death. The king held all the cards.

Esther appears in the story as an orphan. She possesses the gift of great beauty, we are told. But the story neglects to point out that a girl's beauty could also become a liability in the ancient world or anywhere. As I heard a rescued young victim of sex trafficking from Romania say, "The men look at the beautiful girls and see dollar signs in their eyes."

After her heroic cousin, Mordecai, takes in the young, beautiful orphan Esther, the king issues an edict. All the fair virgins in the land were to be rounded up by soldiers for a mandatory beauty contest. Esther was one. The adventure begins. After a long regime of beauty treatments, Esther spends a series of nights going into the king's quarters to spend the night with him, which is part of the contest. We are left to wonder what happens to her overnight. However, she won the king's favor and became the fairest in the land. He made her his new queen, replacing Vashti, the one he banished.

All seems to be well, but there's a catch. Esther had not revealed her true identity to the king. She pretended to be a Gentile to enter into the contest when she was a Jew. We understand that this was because her people were in danger. The king had promoted a man, Haman, to be the prime minister who was plotting to assassinate the Jews. Esther's uncle found out about it and got word to her through the royal court's walls. He told her she must save her people. But to do this, she would have to risk her life, not only revealing her true identity to the king but by visiting him unsummoned to make her request.

Well, it all worked out. Because of the king's great love and adoration of Esther, she exposed the plot, the king hung his prime minister on the gallows, and Esther was praised for her bravery. Several more layers unfold, including a bloody battle and victory for the Jews. But perhaps we've missed a few important details in the story.

Abandonment Is Real

Two women were abandoned in this story. The first is Queen Vashti, who refused to appear before the king when she was summoned to his banquet. He wished to show off her legendary beauty to his guests; in other words, he was intoxicated and wanted to parade her before his male dinner guests like a trophy. She refused to appear, so he banished her from his kingdom. We don't know where she went; she was written out of the story.

The second woman is Esther. She was first abandoned by her parents, then by Mordecai, as he allowed her to be rounded up for the mandatory beauty contest rather than protecting her from such a brutal affair. In Esther, Mordecai saw an opportunity. It was a chance for him to gain a foothold into the kingdom's inner circle and, of course, have an opportunity to save his people, which is the point of the story.

We can certainly celebrate that Esther indeed came into power for "such a time as this," which is the famous quote from the story. And indeed, she had a critical role to play at a time when people's lives were at stake. But we don't often look beyond the circumstances in which she remained trapped. Esther freed her people, but could she save herself? As long as she was the queen, she would be subject to the king's whims. And he had proven to dispose of women when they refused to obey his will.

Violence Against Women—A True Story

As we peel back the layers of Esther's story, it helps us to understand the insanity that fuels a culture of violence against women. We so often want to paint the story of a powerful woman who saves her people because that is wonderful and magical. And that is a thing to be celebrated. But we often overlook the little pieces of the story that are deeply disturbing. We miss the details that involve Esther's personal life. Such as being part of a group of young women forcefully taken by the king's soldiers. Esther didn't have a choice. She was a prisoner from the start. The only option she had once she was behind the kingdom's walls was to go further in and gain as much power as she could as a victim.

The fact that Mordecai took Esther in as an orphan tells us she had no way of providing for herself. He didn't hide her away or seek to protect her. Esther was forced to save the pieces of herself that she could while working within the dysfunctional system that is the bedrock of the story. Esther may be a hero, but she is also a survivor. She was forced by fate to develop survival skills in a system that made her a victim. She learned how to do the best she could in a sick system.

Violence against women is rarely random. It's been developed systematically over thousands of years. That's precisely the reason why it's so difficult to eradicate. People prosper from the victimization and abandonment of women. It happens all over the world on various levels.

At the bottom of the system, we see young girls being sold into sex trafficking by the people they trust: parents, guardians, friends, or relatives. There are thousands of different stories. In India, for example, the practice of selling young girls into temple prostitution is still alive, often generated by poverty. The women do the best they can in this system, sometimes even organizing in groups to educate one another on safe sex practices. But they rarely escape the system.

The religious teaching that women are supposed to be obedient to men often sets girls up for all kinds of disasters. As victims of violence know, not all men have good intentions, just to name one reason. For example, in a community where women are supposed to be obedient to men, there will often be a woman with a story about how a male religious authority figure sexually violated her. Or how as a girl, a leader of the church molested her, and she was often forced to keep quiet about her story to maintain expectations of obedience to male authority. Or perhaps no one believed she was telling the truth. I've heard many of these stories in women's groups. And, tragically, coming forward and exposing the truth often placed the woman's safety at risk. She might have been banished from her community for telling the truth or have to endure further violence.

Even recently, in American culture, as the #MeToo movement has gained participants, women have risked being rejected, criticized, shamed, fired from a job, and slandered publicly for telling the truth about the violence done to them. You can see how this is psychologically damaging to women. When women are bullied and even threatened into remaining silent about the damages that have been committed against them, it causes a breakdown in a woman's identity, a soul wound. A woman experiences a loss of wholeness when her story is not believed. When women are forced to keep silent for their own survival or reveal their trauma to people who refuse to believe them, they often remain in captivity to their wounds. Sometimes for lifetimes.

Healing and transformation can happen as we hear the lost stories of women from the biblical world. Their stories lead us on a healing journey. They become our empathetic witnesses. And as we learn to read the Bible from a woman's perspective, we learn to trust our own instincts. As we do, we learn to become companions to ourselves and not abandon what is truthful for us.

Untaming the Story

It is difficult to breathe behind the ironclad walls of a story that doesn't fully ring true. We need to tell the true stories no matter who believes them because honesty is the pathway to healing. We need to untame Esther's story so that we can untame our own. Bible stories were never meant to cause us harm. They are with us to show us how God loves us even though we get caught up in the oppressive human schemes of power, greed, manipulation, and control. We are not trapped in the story. God is calling us out to the edges and uncharted pathways to reveal what is true. God's image is in all of us, just waiting for us to have faith in it.

The stories carry within them the pathways of those who sought to follow God within the framework of a particular culture. We all have different cultures that have their very own challenges. Some of us are in more progressive cultures, and some are in very conservative ones. Some of us grow up in abject poverty, while others grow up in immense luxury. But we all need to figure out what honesty means if we are to heal.

God is calling us into healing. Sometimes this means becoming free of a culture that is oppressive for us. Sometimes it means helping those who are in unjust situations. Whatever our circumstances, we will not be helped by dishonesty. If we are willing to do an honest reading of them, Bible stories will lead us to a deeper understanding of the difference between the will of God and the will of humankind. These are not always the same thing, even in the Bible! Wherever we see harm being done to a human soul, male or female, we see that God's love is not in this. It is a choice of the human will to harm. When we can read the stories through the lens of God's unconditional love, then our authentic learning will begin. We will develop discernment and make better decisions for ourselves. It's just one of the many things we learn as we spend time with these wild and holy women of the Bible.

Eventually, we will become free from the wounds and the entrapment of violence. We will learn how to free ourselves and others. We will learn how to follow the story that God has written upon the walls of our souls. It's never too late to get our story straight. But let's not wait any longer.

Reflection

1. Name a time in your life when you felt abandoned. There are many different types of abandonment. There is no right or wrong answer. The important thing is to get in touch with that feeling. Most of us carry a fear of abandonment deep within us. Sometimes the first step in becoming less afraid is to name your fear.

2. If you were abandoned, what did you do to survive? What action did you take? What emotions did you feel when you were abandoned?

3. Has anyone ever taught you that you were inferior to men as a "biblical" teaching? How does this make you feel about God?

4. Has there been a time in your life when you had to make a big decision and you were confused about what you thought? Were you able to make the decision on your own, or did you seek out a male authority figure?

5. Write something about your story today that feels true and honest about how you feel after hearing Esther's story. Share this with a trusted friend.

Journal Space

Ten Thousand Charms

I will rise and wonder the streets,
Looking for the one my soul loves.
Have you seen him?
Dark as a raven
With eyes as soft as doves.

Only in his arms
There are ten thousand charms.

Let me kiss the kiss of his mouth
Until the shadows flee.
Winter's over, the rain is gone;
Now is the time to sing.

O awake, North wind, and come.
Blow upon my garden sweet.
Let its fragrance reach my dear one,
Let him come and deeply drink.

CHAPTER 6

The Beloved

(Song of Songs)

Rather than trying to tame the poem, why not take pleasure in its otherness…?
–Cheryl Exum

The search for love is big business in our culture. It might be impossible to even estimate how many billions of dollars the love industry generates each year. From dating apps to romance novels to perfume to dieting and fitness, so much of our consumer imagination revolves around that ever-dangling fantasy of securing the perfect love.

Like the young woman in the Song of Songs, most of us have searched for love. Maybe we're not as bold as she, chasing down her elusive lover through the streets at midnight. But most of us have done some pretty desperate things in the name of love. We have a love-shaped hole in our hearts, and we're restless until we fill it. But do we know what we are looking for when we're searching for love? And is it true that it's challenging to love others when we have not learned how to love ourselves?

Like the young woman in the Song of Songs poem, we have often searched for love outside of ourselves or in other people. We have chased it down, beckoned it, cried out for it, or tried to give it, and we have often ended up confused about what love is, how it works, and how we find it. We've often allowed others to tell us who we are and thought it was love. Perhaps we have tried to make someone else the object of a love we felt unable to access in ourselves. Or maybe we've given ourselves away to people who weren't available as we tried desperately to be loved.

We've been loved with an imperfect love. Of course, we are all imperfect. But if we grew up thinking that love is being shamed or were told that we are not good enough, then we may have developed an unhealthy image of love. Someone may have betrayed us and called it love. Someone may have sexually abused us and convinced us it was love. It's okay to be confused about love! We may find ourselves in need of some direction when it comes to experiencing life-giving love. Song of Songs is a beautiful book to guide us into a greater sense of that Divine love we have inside.

Searching and Not Finding

Many of us can relate to the woman in the Song of Songs Chapter 3:1–3:

> *On my bed nightly*
> *I have sought my soul's beloved*
> *I sought him, but I did not find him.*
> *I will rise now and go about the city.*
> *In the streets and in the squares:*
> *I will seek my soul's beloved*

I sought him, but I did not find him.
The watchmen found me.
Those who go the rounds of the city
My soul's beloved—have you seen him?

We are all searching for our beloved. It seems that the love-shaped hole inside of us doesn't stop aching until we find something to feed it. We go searching for someone or something to fill this void inside. We have a driving desire for love, affection, and acceptance. After all, love is a basic need. It's not as if it's something we can live without! However, it can sometimes be confusing when we find that the object of our affection, be it a person or a dream fulfilled, may not make the void disappear. We may be confused if we still feel an emptiness. It may subside a bit when we are busy or in the heat of a relationship, but if a sense of emptiness returns, it can leave us bewildered. We may have a feeling that something is missing that we can't quite name. We may have spent a lifetime trying to fill this hole with substitutes like drugs, alcohol, excitement, or distraction. But there is still a Divine love inside of us all, waiting to be our companion.

Tending Your Vineyard

Song of Songs is an untamed poem about love and narrates the experience of love from both a male and a female perspective. It contains vivid images of love and desire, as you can readily see in the song "Ten Thousand Charms". I used the biblical text to compose the song.

There are a few central themes throughout this book of love, and these pop up in our own lives, too, including the pursuit of love and its mysterious disappearance. We can also relate to the theme of the confusion that follows when one's love for another is not returned. Another theme is the ecstasy of love's embrace when it is mutually experienced. We also hear something we want to believe: that love is as strong as death, and love has conquered even the grave.

The Song of Songs is a radical poem for the Bible. According to its title, it is the "best of the best," the Song of *all* Songs. It's a conversation between a woman and a man. But what's radical about it is that the woman is the one who is the pursuer. She is searching the streets at night, begging the watchmen to show her where her beloved has gone. She will be restless until she finds him and has laid possession to his love, his kisses, and his embrace. She is incomplete without him and feels empty and directionless. According to the poem, he is her reason for being, and he is the mirror image of her beauty, which is unique and rare among all women.

Yet, there are a couple of haunting refrains in the poem that resonate with me. She seems certain that her lover holds the key to her completeness. Yet, she lets a couple of statements fly that leave the reader wondering if there might be another untraveled pathway that her heart desires. A hidden inner garden that she has not been allowed to access. In chapter 1:6, she reveals, "My mother's sons were angry with me, they made me keeper of the vineyards, my own vineyard I have not kept."

My own vineyard I have not kept. How many of us spend our lives tending to the needs of others while the life inside of us is put on hold? How many of our own vineyards have been neglected? What would our lives look like if we had the time, presence, focus, and permission to tend our own vineyards? Is that even a possibility?

Women are often conditioned into codependency, set up from the start. A very basic definition of codependence is "focusing on the wants and needs of others rather than our own."[36]

When a woman is taught to believe that other's needs are more important than her own, she learns that love is something primarily done for others. Serving others who are in need is undoubtedly a part of love's fruits and a pathway to meaning and purpose. Being in a vocation where a large part of my job is serving those in need has taught me that service is a pathway to healing and a meaningful life. But it took a long time for me to understand that giving service to others in a codependent way might be helpful to others but it was draining me. As long as I paid more attention to the needs of others than I did to my own needs, I found myself severely fatigued, with little left to give at the end of the day.

It's as simple as the instructions the airline attendant demonstrates at the beginning of each flight: "Make sure you put the oxygen mask on your own face before trying to put it on the face of someone else." We each need to help ourselves breathe first. As we learn to love and esteem ourselves, we begin to tend to the Divine love within us. We are filled with the energy and spiritual force we need to go out and help others. But in active codependence, this is difficult to do. In this mindset, it isn't easy to do simple things to take care of ourselves because we believe, in a codependent state, that we can only find out who we are by putting others' needs first. Though it may be difficult, it is possible to unlearn codependent behavior and learn to sustain ourselves with a greater love.

Indeed, this is a necessary process for the healthy development of a sense of self apart from others. We each need to form a healthy individuality so that we can comprehend this relationship between our unique self and God's Divine presence in us. From the Song of Songs, we see that the woman is seeking her soul's beloved. She will only be complete when she takes possession of him. She is tortured until she finds him. But there is another haunting refrain in this poem that is repeated: "Do not arouse or awaken love before it wishes." Love is in charge, and when love awakens, it pushes us to act. But if we act too soon, it can be a frightening dance.

Many have heard beauty in this poem, and I have as well. But there's also something else that I hear - a woman searching for her own identity in the pursuit of a male partner. I hear that this relentless pursuit destabilizes her and makes her take risks that are dangerous as she roams the streets at night, alone, searching for her lover.

While the love poetry itself is exquisitely beautiful and lush, full of images of the purity and uniqueness of love, I see another angle. One angle doesn't cancel out the other; it just gives us another insight. Love can be destabilizing if we are searching for ourselves in another person. As women, many of us have been conditioned to deny ourselves in order to be of service to others. It's not wrong to love and serve others; of course, this is how we live out of the faith that we exist for something greater than ourselves. But when we do so at the expense of never having taken the opportunity to "tend to our own vineyards," it can become destabilizing. There is love within us that seeks to grow, an inner beloved calling us to dance. As our inner vineyard grows, we have more energy to share ourselves and our gifts with the greater world around us. We connect with what gives us life abundant, God's love within us all.

You Are Beloved

Everyone indeed goes through some wounding in this life. Still, certain wounds tear at our identity in such a way that it destabilizes us at our very core. When a woman is violated, she experiences a wounding at the spiritual level. Some call it a soul tear. It is a spiritual wound to our wholeness. But this rupture can also become a seed of our healing.[37]

We can heal from these kinds of wounds, and love is the medicine. Love applied to us from our Creator. Friar Thomas Keating has called it "Divine Therapy."[38] The Song of Songs can lead us down a healing pathway as we apply this poem to the pursuit of our inner life.

The woman of the Song of Songs is seeking her soul's beloved. "I am my beloved, and my beloved is mine" (6:3). The word *beloved* means "dear to the heart." What would it mean to become beloved to God within? To cherish the inner child, the inner person, or the one who God has created.

You have likely heard the saying, "You can't love another person until you learn to love yourself." I don't know if this is entirely true, but there is truth in it. Love is a lifetime endeavor. We reach new levels of God's love as we learn to love ourselves and others. God's love is endless within us and deep beyond our comprehension. We come to know it as we allow ourselves to receive healthy love, and even though it may seem awkward, as we tell ourselves, we *are* loved. Affirmations in the mirror may seem strange at first, but staring into one's own eyes and telling oneself, "I love you" each day can work wonders.

We don't need to chase love to tend our own vineyards. Love will grow inside of us as we make this decision. Love will liberate us as we decide to shine it into our lives. After all, love truly is the most powerful force in the universe. As we come to know this greater love within ourselves, it heals us and enables us to extend a stable love for others. Our relationships with others benefit as our soul's beloved is nurtured.

Reflection

1. Do you feel that you have to take care of others so much that it causes your own life to feel unstable?

2. Name a time when you felt that you lost some of your own identity just to give love to another person.

3. Name a time when you felt at one with God and yourself. Were you alone? What were you doing? What was special about that moment?

4. Name something you really love about yourself. Is this something that is a gift from God? How can you develop this something you love about yourself?

5. Affirmations are a powerful tool to help you bring awareness to the beloved within. I've listed some prayer and affirmation exercises that you can practice to connect with the inner beloved at the end of Chapter 7 (p. 97). Try these out and write some reflections in your journal after you've tried the practices. What changes have you noticed? How do you feel after trying them?

Journal Space

Virgin Mirror

They all come to me in the end,
Powerful men;
Though they are kings, they cannot summon
The truth. It's in the wind,
the truth is in the wind.
I see the dead, not the living,
But in the living man's eyes
I thought I recognized a friend:
Scared to live, afraid to die, scared to live.
He was broken.

Like a virgin mirror, a virgin mirror.
He held up to his heart
Like the strings, the once soothing strings
Of David's harp, the strings of David's harp.
Broken.

We come together in the end,
The disenfranchised and the powerful men
And wonder why God's blessing
Chose others to befriend.
I guess the truth is in the wind.
All you can do is gather your strength
And hold your head up high.
Let me take care of you tonight,
I can see you've been broken.

Oh, you wanna hear your soul sing,
But you're haunted by the breaking,
the moment of the breaking,
the moment of the breaking...

Chapter 7

The Medium of Endor

(1 Samuel 28:3–25)

*To say that I am made in the image of God is
to say that love is the reason for my existence,
for God is love.*
−Thomas Merton

E lizabeth Bishop's poem "The River Man" tells of a man who desired to be more than merely human. Living in a remote Amazonian village, among one of the many tribes, he was becoming a witch doctor who worked with water spirits. In his visions, he was taken beneath the river into the spirit world. The spirits led him into many rooms and showed him the cure for diseases. Yet, he had a hard time comprehending what was happening to him. He longed to learn to recognize the spirits leading him there, and he wanted to capture their image. He began searching for "a virgin mirror no one's ever looked at, that's never looked back at anyone, to flash up the spirits' eyes."[39]

Of course, his frustration grew as he realized he couldn't find a pure mirror because every time he tried to find one, someone had already looked into it. It was impossible to see the spirits' reflection because of the many images the mirrors had already captured.

It's hard for us to picture the image of God. Each time we look into the mirror, we see our faces, hair, bodies, and physical image. How can the image of God be within us? When we gaze at our reflection, what do we see? Do we take the time to tell ourselves, "I love you"? Or do we fret over surface things like lines, features, a nose we don't like, or eyebrows that seem too thin? What do we see of our image that represents God within us? If the mirror could repeat our thoughts, we might be horrified. Indeed there are no "virgin mirrors." Perhaps the image of God is not something a mirror can capture. We don't need to see proof to know that God is there, but we do need something like a healing process to connect with it at times. Because life has given us enough wounds to make us doubt that we are made of God's love. Sometimes these wounds have a voice. We often hear it speaking when we look in the mirror, but is it possible to listen to the voice of love instead?

It can seem difficult to change the messages we speak to ourselves or to alter our internal dialogue. The core belief that women are inferior to men has been around a very long time in some of our world's foundational belief systems. This belief may even become a part of our self-image. In Christianity, the church fathers created a narrative about women based on their cultural lens. St. Augustine wrote that woman was created to be man's helpmate and that "she is not the image of God, but as far as man is concerned, he is by himself the image of God."[40] This belief has been cycling through Western Christianity for centuries. With these beliefs about women's inferiority remaining so dominant, it's been difficult to conceive of what an image of God might be that reflected the feminine.

Women need an alternative to an exclusively male filter for our spiritual journey. We need to conjure from the depths of our very souls the image of God within the feminine body. We need to learn from it and learn to speak its language, which is love, compassion, forgiveness, curiosity, imagination, and trust for the self as well as others. Out of the depths of our very own souls, we find the pathway forward. God has already placed it there in advance. Deep inner wisdom is available to us all. Maybe we just need a good story to help us see that this image of God within us all is not dead, only sleeping.

The Medium of Endor

The story of Saul and the Medium of Endor helps us find a navigation point; after all, a good story can point the way. She is known as a conjurer in the ancient world. To conjure is to imagine, to appeal to or change, to bring into existence as if by magic. Women are natural conjurers of all kinds of things on this earth. We pull love up from nowhere to sacrifice ourselves for others. We see the good in horrible circumstances; we nurture, protect and summon strength and courage from the depths of ourselves to make the world a better place. Sometimes we create what is not even there just to make life livable. Although the Medium of Endor was known for conjuring the spirits of the dead, she used her skills to bring something more into the story: kindness and honesty. Qualities that had apparently become rare among the people of God.

Though King Saul employed diviners, prophets, and those who read the signs to determine the will of God, he banished all those who practiced conjuring the dead, otherwise known as necromancers. He believed that this ancient practice was a sin and unorthodox. But when Saul's back was up against the wall, he sought her, the Medium of Endor. A woman who was skilled at conjuring the souls of the dead. He needed her to help him find the truth. Something had gone missing from him, a blessing, God's anointing that had enabled him to become the king. It was no longer upon him, and he couldn't seem to get answers from anyone as to why.

Saul had lost God's favor. Even his trusted mentor, Samuel, had gone behind his back and anointed David, a lowly shepherd boy, to displace Saul and become the king. Saul knew that some power had left him, but he couldn't get any answers from anyone. He felt he was going mad. He even tried to kill David!

He consulted all of his royal prophets, dream interpreters, and the Urim, but none of them had answers. So he decided to see the Medium of Endor in hopes that she could conjure the ghost of his beloved mentor, Samuel, who had recently died. He needed to know what was going on.

Under cover of night, he visited her. She refused his request at first because, of course, it was King Saul himself who had made the practice of conjuring the dead an act that was punishable by death. But he assured her she was safe. She did as he requested and conjured Samuel's ghost. A little annoyed for being awakened from his slumber in the afterlife, Samuel informed Saul that he had lost all his anointing and would die in battle the next day. He went on to say that David, God's new choice, would take over the throne.

Saul was in shock when he heard the news. But instead of kicking him out, the medium kindheartedly summoned her servants. She instructed them to prepare a royal meal. Not only had she risked her life to fetch the truth for him, but she showed him kindness in his vulnerable state. The very next day, Saul did die in battle. The very woman he banished to the edges of the kingdom was the one person Saul needed in his darkest hour. She alone pulled the fragmented pieces of Saul's soul back together with her kindness.

Conjuring Wholeness

Women often need to practice conjuring the essential pieces of ourselves that feel lifeless within. This includes our identities, dreams, and purpose, among other things. We need to practice reviving these aspects of ourselves even though it might feel as if we are trespassing on our own property. As we do, we will reach a quiet place within, the place where we feel we might, at last, be able to connect with our true nature. We may have been banished to the edges of our own souls because of violence done to us. We may have convinced ourselves that we are not allowed to meditate, be silent, or go searching for what is whole. We may have been told that we are not worthy of this kind of lavish time and attention. Our time, we may feel, often belongs to others. But we must reclaim it even at the edges of our stories. We need to conjure what has gone missing inside of ourselves and hear what it has to say to us. We need to honor ourselves enough to show kindness and search for the truth.

It is not likely that someone will come knocking on our door to walk us through it. It's not magic either, but instead, it's just communing with God. We can learn to trust that God is within us, at rest and at peace. God is waiting for us to come and abide there too.

We can't dwell in that space all the time, but taking some time each day to talk to yourself and to look at your eyeballs in the mirror and say "I love you" is vital. It's so important to lie on the floor with soft music playing, place our hands over our hearts, breathe deeply, and ask God to come and speak to us. It's imperative to seek to serve what is greater within us while we sort through the world's needs around us. We are all mediums, not of the spirits of the dead, but of the Living One inside of us all. The image of God is within, just waiting to awaken and show us the beauty of Divine love.

Of course, we are not conjuring God; rather, we are seeking a connection. God is often unfathomable, mysterious, and certainly not under our control. But with an attitude of humility and reverence, there are some ways we can connect with God that are accessible to us. It's also a reality that some people who have been wounded may have negative images of God and find themselves asking, "If God loved me so much, why did He let terrible things happen to me?" I am certainly not here to talk you out of your anger or frustration with God. I am only here to provide ways that, when you are ready; you might be able to make some contact with a healing presence within you. Some people have different names for God. Some say Higher Power or Creator or Love. You do not have to call God by the name that feels hurtful or anxiety-producing for you. When you're ready, try some of the exercises below and see if they might work for you in connecting with the image of God within.

Exercises

1. Affirmations. Here are more daily affirmations you can try in front of a mirror. It may feel very awkward at first to do these, but it works if you work it!

   Look at your eyes in the mirror and say, "I love you," "I forgive you," "I believe in you," "I support you," or "I am here for you." Basically all those things you would say to a loving partner to show them you care.

   Try saying those things to yourself over a period of days and observe how you change.

2. Centering Prayer. Centering prayer is an ancient practice. It's very easy to do.

   Take 10 to 20 minutes and sit or lie in a comfortable position. Begin breathing deeply and slowly. Choose a word that represents God; it can be "love," "Creator," "peace," or whatever it is that you feel you are needing to connect to. Each time you complete a cycle of breathing in and breathing out say the word in your mind.

   Keep saying it as you slowly breathe in and slowly breathe out. Make your breaths deep and long at first, and then you will naturally begin to breathe normally. Try it once a day and observe how it changes you.

3. Making something tangible.

   God gives us gifts so that we can connect to God. We often think of our gifts as being ways to get rich or famous, but gifts are not necessarily about what we achieve. Rather, they are useful pathways that connect us to the Divine. As we use them to make things out of our creativity, we feel more connected to the Divine energy of the Creator inside of us all. Maybe there are hidden gifts inside of you that feel dead and in need of conjuring.

Try some simple things to find them. If you feel drawn to pottery, sign up for a pottery class. If you feel led towards the stars, join a star-watching group. If you feel inspired by music, learn to play an instrument or take singing lessons. If you love to write, develop your writing.

The point is we need to create tangible things out of our inspiration. As we do we will find a pathway of creativity that helps to ground us in what is greater than ourselves and connects us to God's creative energy flowing through us all. If it leads to something that supports you, bravo! If not, it's no big deal. Just enjoy it. Enjoy the journey of getting to know what God has put inside of you to be found and loved.

Journal Space

Circling the Godless City

We were made to praise our creator;
Even in our death a praise.
We go against ourselves in this endeavor,
And against each other, it's our way.
All you can do is...
Sing over it all,
Sing to tame the ghosts of the fall,
Sing over it all.

Over all the defenseless,
Working jobs that rob human dignity.
The woman of question
Doin' the dirty deeds to feed her family.
Are God's men circling the Godless city?
Lookin' for me?

You must have heard my song,
Heard that I'm the one
Who makes love from war.
A woman of repute, still I have dreamed of the day
When I would pay for mercy no more.
Could that day be here?
I'll hang a red cord from my window in the wall
And I'll come running
with my loved ones when you call.
See me running when the trumpet calls.

Take me with you,
I know these walls are gonna fall.
'Cause God is singing, Singing
Over it all.

CHAPTER 8

Rahab:
Harlot and Hero

(Joshua 2, 6)

Stories hold the world together.
—Michael Meade

"Y ou're a wild mustang," he said. "You'll never be tamed."

I couldn't argue with him. I had chosen to end our eleven-year relationship and leave the life we had built together. A life that wasn't turning out to be very good for either of us. But because I was doing the choosing, I was the one stamped with the label, "wild." I wonder if I would've thought the same about him if he had decided to leave first? Or would I have just assumed he was something as innocuous as unhappy? When a woman trusts her instincts, she risks being labeled with a name that suggests she has gone rogue. "Wild" was better than some of the other words that were hurled my way when I chose to make my own decisions. When he said it, I'll have to admit, I considered it a compliment, though I'm certain it wasn't meant that way.

A few years ago, I visited the deserts of New Mexico, near Albuquerque, where I met wild mustangs for the first time. They were roaming free on Acoma Pueblo land. I locked eyes with them for a few seconds. That's as long as they would allow me to see into the window of their animal souls before diverting their gaze toward the horizon and fidgeting. But even though I only caught their eyes for a few seconds, I knew that look. I've had it all my life. It's a look that said, "I'd like to take off running, but I also find myself craving the caress of your hand. I wonder if I allowed you to touch me, would it cost me my freedom?" Yeah, I was okay with being compared to them. He was dead right.

When a horse is still wild, it's referred to as "unbroken" in its natural state. Its strong will has not yet been tamed. As it's trained and becomes rideable, safe, more predictable, it is then referred to as "broken." If a horse is ridable but still bucks and kicks, then sometimes you hear the offhanded comment, "that horse is only half-broke." Maybe I was only half-broke. I was bucking, kicking, and screaming my way through a relationship with a man who needed me to be fully broken.

Being a target of labeling seems to be a shared experience among women. Whenever a woman asserts her will or exercises her authority, she is often risks being called a derogatory name. "Bossy," "bitch," "whore," and a few other words come to mind. These labels, over time, can build a wall around a woman's soul. The names are meant to push her back, and keep her down.

But they often have the opposite effect. They invigorate her wildness, stoke her determination and strengthen her resolve to carve out a life of her own. To move away, far away, from the labelers. The walls around a woman's soul will eventually come down, one way or another.

Often, these walls of labeling built up around a girl or a woman are to ensure that she remains within the boundaries of what's expected of her. They are often built with the materials of shame and violence. Perhaps the walls are intended to protect girls and keep them from endangering themselves through acting out or stepping outside of the imposed bounds. These walls so often end up doing damage by sealing us off from our identity and wholeness.

When we meet Rahab, we see that she had been forced to live inside the walls of the fortified city of Jericho, and no one was really working that hard to free her from her captivity. She was a survivor, a prostitute. Prostitution is generally not a profession that makes it to the "dream job" list for girls. It's usually something girls and women are forced into to survive. In Rahab's story, we find a woman who not only has a will of her own but wields it to her advantage and the salvation of her family at an opportune moment. As the walls around her fall, she moves from harlot to hero. One of the many female "wild mustangs" of the biblical world.

Be Your Own Hero

Rahab is a perfect example of a woman who was forced into the shameful label of "prostitute." While her name means "broad" in Hebrew, the authors tell us that she was a prostitute. Although prostitution was frowned upon, it wasn't against the law. However, we often remember her more as a harlot than a hero, even though her actions show us that both can live in the same person. Her reputation precedes her. Like so many clever, resourceful, and brave women, Rahab was, first and foremost, a survivor.

She lived inside the thick walls of a fortified city called Jericho. Jericho was a rough place; some might say a godless city. Some scholars believe that Rahab might have been in some indentured servitude relationship with the king of Jericho and forced into prostitution. We're not exactly sure. But we do know that Joshua's spies visited her establishment, which was known as a place where information was exchanged, a business with a reputation for being a brothel. A place frequented by male officers of the city. Joshua's spies visited her, thinking that she would be "in the know." They were trying to gather tactical information as they were planning their conquest of the city. But they were at risk of being discovered by the king's men while they were there. So, taking advantage of an opportune moment in which she held the cards, she did with them what she was so skilled at doing with other men— she made a deal. She negotiated her life and her family's life in exchange for their safety. She would hide them, mislead the king's men as to their whereabouts, and in return, they would spare her and her family's lives when they marched on the city. It worked. As the walls of Jericho came crashing down under Joshua's attack, Rahab hung a red cord out of her window as the agreed-upon signal for her safety. The walls came tumbling down, so the story goes, and Rahab and her family began a new life with the Israelites. Rahab became a free woman that day.

But even though these were godly men, these male spies had not intended to save Rahab. They only wanted to pump her for information. It was Rahab who demanded her freedom and the safety of her family. She stood up for herself, she negotiated the deal, and she took the risk. Even the risk of having faith in their God. If she had not made her case known and negotiated her self-rescue, she would have perished beneath the falling walls with the rest of the godless city. To be saved, she had to believe that her life was worth saving.

Afterward, she had to trust that these men would make good on their promises. She had learned not to trust men. She had become skilled at turning a profit off of their base desires. Trusting them was a new thing, a risk she had to take. The moment was hers, the opportune time had arrived, and she knew it. Even though she had been branded as an "only good for sex" prostitute, she was the one that was saved. God had something extraordinary in store for her: a new future and a new life. But she had to take the risk of believing in it first. The very walls that she lived in would have become a death trap for her if she had not advocated for her own salvation.

Sometimes we need to take the first step when we begin to awaken to the idea that God has something special in store for our lives. When we start to see the sunlight piercing through the cracks in the walls life has built around us, it isn't easy to believe at first. But it is the very light of freedom that calls us to a new future and a new beginning. When we get the first glimpse of our freedom from pain, from a past, or from the brands that have been attached to us by others, we need to believe in it even if we are the only ones. Even if we are still stuck within the walls, eventually, there will be a way out, and clarity will come. God will provide.

Rahab also had to choose to believe that this God was different than all the other gods. This God meant true freedom and not the fake, manipulative kind that had forced her into selling her body for her daily bread. Somehow she knew the difference deep within herself where she had hidden away a tiny treasure of intuition. Perhaps it was her intuition that enabled her to trust these spies of God.

She believed that this God was circling the godless city and was there to save her, whether the spies knew it or not. She acted on faith in something outside the walls of her existence. She became her very own hero.

Wild Belief

We are all haunted by the ghosts of our past. The voices that seek to convince us we are not worth saving. These voices can become crippling loops in our minds and keep us from breaking out of the cycle of self-sabotage. We can't change what people have spoken over us. However, we can turn down the volume of these voices over time and reduce the power they have over us. We can place them in the background as we move forward into new seasons of our lives. Eventually, these voices fade so far in the distance that we forget to remember how crippling they were. Even though it may be an arduous journey, we are up for it, and we can learn how to sing over it all. As we learn to draw on the strength of our inner wisdom that has been with us all along, we begin to understand that finding peace and purpose is the greatest victory of all. We can make beauty out of the ruins we were given and rescue love from the war of words in our minds.

We can learn new narratives from old stories. We can emerge from the walls built around women's voices in the Bible and the world. We can shatter the brands and labels as we write our own stories. With such a high rate of violence against women in our world today, we have a lot of work to do in our faith communities to examine the foundations that have created a culture of harm. The transformation lies in women's stories being told. These stories will cause the walls of shame to crumble.

The truth of the matter is evident in this very story. Though Rahab is branded a prostitute by the narrators of the story and burdened with all of the images of shame surrounding that label, Rahab is the one who experiences liberation. Not by man but by God and her very own undying belief in her worth. She is the woman of Jericho who was given a new lease on life, a new purpose, and a future. The harlot is the one God chooses to save. She is the one who dares to believe she is worth saving, and she is the one who participates in her own rescue.

Rahab is every woman who is surviving and doing what she has to do to live. Her story lives in us too. We have all likely felt at one time or another that we've had to sacrifice pieces of ourselves to survive in this world. But God has been circling the walls around your heart for a lifetime. God has been waiting for the moment to introduce you to your wholeness. We are all Rahab, waving our red cord in the chaos of the battle, with secret information, deals, confidence, and wit. We are all Rahab with our wild belief in ourselves.

Reflection

1. What walls have been built around your life? Which part of the wall are you responsible for? Which part are others responsible for?

2. Can you name three significant experiences in your life that caused walls to be built around your heart?

3. How have you been branded? What names have people called you in the past?

4. In what ways are the names people have called you different from who you really are?

5. If you were being rescued from the walls around your heart, your soul, and your life, what would you do? What is it you dream of doing with your one precious life? What wild belief do you have in yourself?

Exercises

1. Often the pathway to our freedom can be found in the material of our pain. As we sort through it, we learn to grieve our losses, celebrate our victories (no matter how small), and let go of the hold the past has had upon us. As we name our pain and begin to let go, the walls tumble down and God can begin to do something new in our lives. On a separate piece of paper (or lots of paper) draw some large stone blocks. Inside of each block write down something that caused walls to be built around you. It can be an event or the way someone treated you. It can be something you did or something someone did to you.

2. After you finish this exercise, cut out the blocks one by one. Tape or glue them to a large piece of cardboard or poster board. This is the wall that must be dismantled little by little, over time. Take each block, pray over it, and give the pain of it to God. Ask God to show you how to heal from each incident. It may be that you need to make amends to yourself or to another person. Maybe you need to change your behavior or not be around people who are harming you. Maybe you need to seek out a new community of healthy people to help you heal. You will be able to discern it once you put it up on a wall and examine it. God will show you how the walls will

come tumbling down. Give yourself time and be gentle with yourself. Nurture yourself. You may go through many phases of letting go, just make a beginning. It's enough.

Journal Space

Woman King

"Daughter of my blood, I see you.
I know that I have taught you well,"[41]
But the sword is coming for me.
My story will be yours to tell;
Steal the blessing from curse,
Boil the poison down, verse by verse.

Don't ask me why
I was born to be more than just a queen.
When a woman owns her power,
They all want an explanation for these things.
let the story speak
Of the woman king.

The winners write the history.
But I'm not the only one
Banished for her mystery,
Her legacy undone.

But the Spirit will prevail;
Someday the truth will tear through this unholy veil.

We had seven years of peace, seven years of hope,
seven years of freedom.
Just enough to let you see that you are way close to
gates of heaven's kingdom.

CHAPTER 9

Athaliah:
The Woman King

(2 Kings 8–11, 2 Chronicles 22–23)

All sorrows can be borne
if you can put them into a story.
–Karen Blixen

You may have heard it said that whoever controls the narrative has the power. In my school history classes growing up, I learned one dominant narrative as the "American" story. It was the settlement of North America by white colonists that spread from the east to the west. We learned that these colonists conquered the vast wilderness regions west of the east coast, the primitive lands that stood between them and what they called "progress." The big story of how we got to here taught us that colonial settlers sought peace with Native Americans but ultimately felt the need to conquer and Christianize them. As a gesture of so-called "civilization," Native Americans were warehoused in reservations and their children were sent to boarding schools, that is, if they escaped death. This is the history I grew up learning; perhaps you did as well.

However, as I grew older, I was fascinated by different histories. I became drawn to the counter narratives of the dominant stories I was taught. I learned about the wide range of cultures among Native American people. I realized that our histories are intertwined and that there is no singular history. Native American stories also include enslavement, not freedom, and rights being taken away instead of liberty and justice for all. It has been said that the winners write the history. But if we only read what the winners write, we miss out on some essential information. Stories that have been buried beneath the dominant narrative are often the ones that provide missing links to a more honest interpretation. These stories help us to be better people as we learn to embrace, empower and uplift those who have been oppressed.

If we're searching for a more honest version of history, we need to hear all the stories within the narrative—those of the so-called winners and losers, the powerful and powerless. As we hear these stories, we realize we are connected. As we dig into the larger story with honesty and truth, we begin to gain access to our own stories' missing pieces.

It is widely believed that Bible stories were written down by men. Even when we hear women's stories, they are very often portrayed as "supporting characters in a male drama."[42] So, when we read Bible stories, if they are to have their fullest power in our lives, we need to ask questions to get underneath the layers of the dominant lore. Such as: Who is benefitting from this story? Who is in power? Who is oppressed? What is God up to in this story? Where am I in this story?

There is a saying, "Learn to read slow: all other graces will follow in their proper places."[43] When we slow down our reading, we begin to see the stories beneath the stories. We hear the buried voices of the victims, which are often women's voices. We begin to understand what they were up against in having their own stories told, and not just told, but believed.

A woman often fights a million battles to tell her story. First, she has to fight against those in power who have convinced her that her story is unimportant and insignificant. Sometimes this is a tough battle because it's a war waged against the people she loves the most. Then she must learn to distinguish her voice above all the male voices she was taught to obey. This takes a long time, and it's much like tuning a piano with a tuning fork. She has to do it long enough to discern the proper tone, pitch, resonance, and key of her voice. Once she thinks she has found something resembling her voice, she has to risk using it. It's hard at first, and it hurts because it's a new muscle. She gets beaten back a hundred times. She gets violated for even considering using her voice to fight for her rights or the rights of others. She gets bullied for believing in herself. Her soul is wounded, but she continues to fight because she is determined to believe in her one authentic voice. She has fought so long for the voices of others, all while feeling her voice tugging at her, patient but insistent, waiting for the right time to emerge.

It wasn't always safe for women's voices to emerge in the Bible. Still, women spoke up because they were compelled by God, a force much more potent than hatred or oppression. When we encounter the story of Athaliah, it feels like a strange miracle. A woman became an Israelite ruler in the Bible? Yet it's there in plain sight. How could we have missed her story? Her voice and her reign may have been short-lived, but still, she reigned. This is her story.

The Female Monarch

The reign of Athaliah, the woman queen who became king,[44] narrated in 2 Kings 8–11 (and 2 Chronicles 22–23) is a tale of conflicting accounts. There are no questions about whether or not she reigned; that part is clear. What is unclear is whose side she was on. Was she wicked, or was she acting with a clear conscience? It all boils down to who is telling the story.

The fact is, the Bible doesn't give us too many clues about Athaliah's reign. The details of events during her kingship are left out of the story. The biblical authors themselves seem to be confused about Athaliah as if they don't quite know what to make of this powerful woman. It is unclear whether or not she was the daughter of Omri or Ahab (both kings) or if her loyalties were to the God of Israel, Ba'al, or a little of both. What we do know is that she ruled Judah, the southern kingdom, for seven years. While most traditional interpretations paint her as a wicked ruler, recent scholarship suggests that the lines are not clear-cut.[45] Athaliah refuses to fit neatly into good and bad categories.

Being a royal was a bloody affair in the ancient world. It could be prosperous but also dangerous to carry royal blood. One might be murdered for it or promoted to the monarchy—the life of a royal hinged on the alliances that had the most favor and support. Within Israelite religion and politics, which were like two sides of the same coin, it was no different. These differences in interpretation of God's will ultimately divided the once united kingdom under David into two separate kingdoms, the northern and southern, or Israel and Judah. Battles for the power of the throne ensued.

Athaliah's rise to power is a complicated tale. She ruled the southern kingdom, Judah, for seven years after her husband and son, both kings, were murdered. There were battles fought for power in between. She overtook the southern throne, Judah, after her son was killed and reigned as king. The Bible says she ordered that all the royal seed be killed, which meant wiping out any possible claimants to the throne. She succeeded in the massacre except for one baby boy who was the heir to the throne. He was hidden away during the slaughter. When he was seven years old, he was brought out of hiding and presented as the "true" king. At that point, Athaliah was taken into captivity, marched through the horse's gates, and killed by the new regime's sword. The whole city was quiet on the night Athaliah was murdered.

What is truly remarkable about this story is that Athaliah was an Israelite queen who became a king and ruled Judah for seven years which was a longer reign than some male kings before or after her. However, we are told nothing of the events of her seven-year reign. Was it a peaceful seven years? Was it prosperous?

The narrators of Kings judge Athaliah negatively. Did she get in the way of the storyline, which was primarily about God restoring faithful worship to Judah through male rulers? Is it because she was a woman? Wilda C. Gafney points out that though history seeks to paint her as a worshipper of idol gods, she ruled Judah as an Israelite.[46] Athaliah's presence haunts the landscape of this period in the story of God's people.

While Athaliah kept the southern kingdom alive, defended Judah's borders, and was respected and obeyed, the story remains silent about the details of her reign. But perhaps the silence tells us more about the depths of her power than words ever could. Retelling her story is a way of breaking the silence.

Hearing Women's Voices

When we read stories of women in the Bible who rose to power, even though their stories are there in black and white print, we often have a difficult time believing them. For so long, we have been conditioned to think of women in the Bible playing supportive roles in a male-centered story.

For millennia, women living inside of patriarchal systems have often lacked the power to narrate their own stories. It has often been the norm that women are treated as less believable than men. But with Athaliah's voice, we can turn the volume up. We can let her story speak through us. We don't have to qualify her as good or bad. Indeed, she did some horrific things, as did other kings and queens before and after her. We can simply acknowledge her character in the story as one that has been overlooked. We can tell her story to future generations of girls who might be wondering where all the women who rose to power in the Bible are hidden.

Your Story Belongs to You

When we tell our stories, we often feel that we can't tell the whole truth because the truth sometimes puts us at risk. We may hold in the secrets of our mistreatments because we are afraid if we let them out, we might lose a friend, family member, community, or even lose our own identity. But our stories are who we are and can't be taken from us. As I heard author Anne Lamott say in an interview, "your story belongs to you, and you get to tell it; it's your property."

It's challenging to move beyond our wounds until we can give words to our stories, even if it is just to one or two trustworthy listeners. Putting words into the great chasm of loss can often give us the traction we need to move out of our pain. If something terrible has been done to us, we need to name that too. It's the naming that enables the sting to subside. When we tell the lost stories of women in the Bible, what was previously foggy in our own stories becomes clearer. We begin to take ownership of what happened to us. And as we do, we gain the power to become the authors of our lives.

The pen is now in your hands. Let me help you write your story. Together we will steal the blessing from the curse and learn how to let your story speak.

Descansos is the practice of placing a cross at roadside memorials where someone has died. Author Clarissa Pinkola Estes (*Women Who Run with the Wolves: Myths & Stories of the Wild Woman Archetype*) has spoken of the practice of doing descansos over the losses of one's own life.[47] She explains how to chart a timeline of your life across a horizontal sheet of paper or poster and draw a cross in those years in which you experienced a loss of wholeness or identity. Beside the cross or in a journal, you write down the loss and how you felt about it. (Detailed instructions are in the exercises below). You may need more space in a journal to write down your feelings about the event. It can be something violent that was done to you, or it could be a loss due to someone who left you or was taken from you. Think of a moment in which something inside of you felt as if it died.

It's important to mark these moments because these little crosses become places where the treasure is buried, covered in our pain. We can reclaim these moments of little, mini deaths for our resurrection. "Little girl, rise up!"

Just as Jesus did for the people he healed, we need to name the things that have caused us to feel unalive. Marking them as they have marked us, so we might claim what has become lost in us, wholeness itself. We are the rightful heirs of the Divine image of God within. But it is up to us to claim it and to move out of the victim narrative that has trapped us for so long. The naming causes the pain to lose its power over us.

You are not written out of your own story; you are a story yet to be written. As the bindings of your pain fall off, read what is written there and let the story be your pathway to resurrection.

Reflection

1. Let's try an exercise of descansos.

   On a piece of paper, poster or in a journal, make a timeline. Choose a period of your life because charting your whole life at once might be overwhelming. Maybe choose a period of your childhood, teenage years, or adult years in which things were painful, or go with a period you don't remember very well.

   Now chart this period with the years of your life (or months). Draw a cross within a period of time in which something happened to you that was particularly painful. Underneath the cross write a few words to explain what happened. You can do this for any time period of your life. If you want to, chart it on a long banner. You can tape together pieces of paper or purchase a banner. You can put it up on your wall and chart your lifeline.

   As you recall things that happened to you, you can write them in with a cross on each significant event in which you felt an extreme sense of loss. Take your time; you can leave the banner up as you make your way through this book.

2. Say a prayer over each loss. It can be a very simple prayer and it can be to the God of your understanding. A Higher Power, the Divine One. You can write a simple prayer, such as a mantra of loss,

that you say over each one. Keep it reverent and simple. Something like this below, or you can use this one.

"God, I know that I experienced a great loss in this moment. I trust that you are with me now as I seek healing from this loss. I seek to understand your wisdom, and I seek grace and forgiveness for myself. Mostly I seek healing for the damage, the wounds, and the pain that it caused. Show me the pathway to my own healing so that I might experience your light, love, and peace."

3. In a separate place write a little piece of your own story. How did this loss make you feel? What exactly do you feel was taken from you? How did this loss hurt others? Ask these questions: How have I experienced healing from this loss? What am I afraid of because of this loss? What could I say to others about this loss that would help them with a similar pain? Try this exercise with each cross you place on your descansos timeline. See where it leads you.

Journal Space

In My Lover's Arms

Today, I wish I were a dove
Soaring in the mountains of my youth,
Dreaming of falling in love
With the man, the man that I would choose.

In my lover's arms, you can do me no harm,
In my lover's arms you can me no harm.

Father, what have you done?
Family claims another victim.
Trust is such an easy word to say,
But the bridges between us lie hidden.

In my lover's arms, you can do me no harm,
In the fortress of my lover's arms
you can do me no harm.

CHAPTER 10

Jephthah's Daughter: The Wanderer

(Judges 11)

*Story is meant to set the inner life
back into motion again.*
–Clarissa Pinkola Estes

When I was a young girl, I lived at the edge of a forest. I spent a lot of time there pretending and playing, listening to the brook, the birds, and the animals darting across the forest floor. Though I was in the woods alone, I never felt lonely. I felt like me; comfortable, natural, and uninhibited. In this realm at the edge of civilization, I crossed that liminal space of expectations, chores, rules, and limits and was free. At least until dark when my mother called me in for bedtime. I was always within earshot of home.

As an adult, I became aware of significant traumatic experiences that occurred in my life. Even though I was consciously aware of what happened, I had never processed the pain, fear, and helplessness I felt. These emotions were still frozen inside of me, waiting to be expressed and released.

When I began a recovery process, my inner child longed to be back in the woods. I knew that the forest would be a place of healing for me. I began to search for a camper I could park somewhere and had this idea that I would leave civilization and go live in the woods until I was healed. The idea of processing my feelings seemed so overwhelming that I felt only the vast expanse of nature could hold me. I took cash out of the bank and began looking at refurbished vintage campers. As I followed through on the fantasy, I realized that the campers I could afford made me feel claustrophobic, and spending the night in the woods alone wasn't the same as wandering in the forest in daylight.

After going through with the urge, I eventually decided that I didn't really need to live in the woods alone; I just wanted to see what it felt like to give myself that kind of freedom. I put the money back in the bank and took lots of hikes. I had the urge to wander, and I couldn't deny it; to roam in the forest alone, just being, listening, and feeling safe. But of course, the world had changed significantly. I no longer felt safe in the woods like I did as a child. I lived in the city; I wasn't near any large swaths of the wilderness. So I drove to hiking trails and carried a hunting knife with my big dog at my side. Giving myself the space to roam was important. A woman needs room to roam, even if she answers the call to come back home at the end of the day.

When I read the story of Jephthah's daughter, I felt as if my inner child was reading it through me. So much of the scholarship about this story focuses on the violence of it. A young girl is sacrificed by her father because of a rogue promise he made to God. He is a male hero while his daughter becomes the sacrificial lamb. It's a violent story in a book where most women are not safe—a book in which society has completely unraveled. The daughters are rarely secure, not even in their own homes. Jephthah's daughter becomes a target, a scapegoat for the sickness of a society gone mad. As violence and blame are placed upon the daughters, society can pretend that nothing is wrong and go about the business of dysfunction. Mieke Bal states: "the virgin daughter has to pay with her life for the society's incapacity to solve the conflicts."[48]

I've stared at this angle for a long time. I wanted to tell myself that I, too, was disposable because I carried around a lot of pain from experiences in which I felt like a scapegoat. But something about her request gave me pause and led me in a new direction. She took agency in the story and asked for what she needed. Somehow, she had the presence of mind to do that, even facing her imminent death at the hands of her own father. Her only request was to roam in the mountains for two months before he carried out the unfathomable deed of sacrificing her. He gave her permission, and she was off to the wilderness. I explored the violence in this story and my own for so long that I began to see something new. Her desire to wander in the wilderness was the doorway to her salvation. There she could have the experience of her soul's wandering, freely, without being hunted. Cradled in the arms of the wild, her lover's arms, nature itself became her healer.

Let Me Go and Roam the Mountains

She is not even given a name. She was young, perhaps an early teenager. She had not yet been betrothed in marriage. Jephthah, her father, was a man who had grown up in a dysfunctional family system. He was bullied out of his home as a boy by his brothers once they found out he was the son of a prostitute. His half-brothers convinced him he would not inherit anything from his father, and they forced him to run away.

Jephthah grew up as a homeless boy, his family a gang of outlaws. He was raised to be intimidating, and he was good at it. However, he was, by his father, Gilead, still technically an Israelite. So when the Ammonite army threatened the tribes of Israel, they conveniently remembered Jephthah; he was one of them. They set him loose as their fearless leader upon the mighty Ammonite army, equipped only with a lifetime of pain and survival skills.

Jephthah made preparations to pursue the Ammonite army. Perhaps he kept hearing in the back of his mind the statements the Israelite elders had made to him. "If you are victorious, you will be our leader." This was the promise. There would be acceptance at last and power and prestige if he won. He would be someone again; he would belong. The family who kicked him out would have to accept that he was the most powerful man in the land. He would, at last, have a place in his rightful family. So Jephthah prayed. He made a vow with God that if God helped him win the battle, he would sacrifice the first living thing that greeted him upon his return home.

Now Jephthah may not have known about the Spirit of the Lord when it came upon him to walk with him in the battle.

Perhaps he didn't know how to read the signs. It was what we might call a good omen. But why would the Spirit of the Lord come upon him? After all, the Lord's people had kicked him out as a young boy and left him for dead. Why would he be favored?

This kind of thing might have required Jephthah to trust God. Something he was supposed to have learned from his family of origin. But since they mistreated him so harshly, he had learned the opposite, to be suspicious of love, maybe even suspicious of the God of his people. He was shown by example that the ones who love you, the ones you are dependent upon for your basic needs as a child, can also leave you for dead. Especially if you don't represent the values upheld in their belief system. He had learned as a young boy what the world is about: survival insured by violence. These two things accompanied one another in the world he had come to know. So he made a deal with God, won the battle, and when he returned home, the living thing that greeted him was his daughter, dancing to celebrate his victory.

As soon as Jephthah saw his daughter, he remembered his promise to God and tore his clothes, an act of grief and distress. He was deeply grieved that he would now have to sacrifice his daughter to fulfill his promise to God. He failed to see any way out of it. He explained the situation to his daughter. She had only one request, to roam the wilderness with her companions for two months and to grieve. She wanted to mourn the life she would not be allowed to live. Maybe she could have stayed in the mountains forever or run away, but she returned home, and we assume the deed was done.

It reminds us of another story, when Abraham was told that he would have to sacrifice his son, Isaac, upon an altar. As Abraham was about to take the knife to Isaac, God intervened and stopped it. Isaac's life was saved, but Jephthah's daughter's life was not. Is this the way it was really meant to be? Do the authors of the Bible intend through both of these stories to send us the message that male lives are a priority, while female lives are not? Are girls disposable while boys are sacred? But something has gone wrong with Jephthah and his daughter. A dysfunctional system has caused the world to turn upside down. Perhaps this is the story of a world gone awry and people doing as they please, where up is down. Yet we understand this world; it's where we live, too. Violence, family dysfunction, and generational trauma are part of our lives too. We don't escape this in the Bible or in the daily lives we lead. It makes the spiritual practice of wandering even more appealing.

The Art of Wandering

I once had a mentor who taught me the concept of the bummel. It means to stroll, saunter, to wander around at a leisurely pace with no particular destination in mind. To drive slowly down a country road, to walk meditatively through the woods. To take a day to be. I've since tried to practice this as a spiritual discipline. It feels odd at first, but once you get into the habit, it seems necessary. Wandering is a lost art.

Roaming gives the body time to let the memories and hauntings deep down in the bones come out to the surface in the safe cradle of creation itself. We need to give our bodies time to process painful experiences or just to let the joy of nature sink into our bones. This seems to be at the heart of the daughter's request. Her death was hastened much earlier than ours, but it's still a destination on all of our horizons. Let's roam a little before then. Spend a few nights under a full moon with nothing between you and the heavens but the canvas of a tent. Make a fire outside and spend hours being mesmerized by the crackle and popping of dead wood. Wander.

The daughter's desire to roam in the mountains calls out to that still wild place within us all, that untamed story waiting to be lived in our very souls. The healing journey that awaits us is also a wandering in a wilderness of transformation. Know that however lonely you may feel, however sad, disoriented, and confused you may become, these women have walked the path before you and held the hand of God; you can too. So, go ahead, follow these women into the still-wild places of your very own heart. When you finally answer the call home, it will be sweeter than ever before.

Exercises

1. Read the story in Judges 11. I recommend going to www.biblegateway.com and searching for the translation called The Message. After reading the story, write a letter to Jephthah's daughter in the journal section. Ask her the questions that are on your mind, questions you might ask your own inner child if she had been through something this traumatic.

2. With your non-dominant hand answer the letter in your journal as if you were Jephthah's daughter. It's okay if it looks like scribbling. We usually don't write well with our non-dominant hand, but good handwriting is not the goal. The goal is discovery. Don't think about it too much, just write down what comes to you.

3. What did you discover about yourself in this exercise? Was there any new or surprising information?

4. This is a process called "non-dominant handwriting" and it's used widely to help people heal through inner inquiry. We are often sealed off from our feelings and using the non-dominant hand to dialogue with your "inner wisdom" or your "inner child" is a great way to get in touch with your feelings. There are some wonderful resources out there on non-dominant handwriting. I encourage you to do some research or talk to a licensed therapist about the process before diving into it too deeply.

Journal Space

ACKNOWLEDGMENTS

First of all, I'd like to thank all the female Bible scholars whose devoted work brought these stories into my life. There have been so many, but I'd like to name a few whose writing has been particularly formative for me. Esther Fuchs, Mieke Bal, Johanna W.H. van Wijk-Bos, Wilda Gafney, Tikva Frymer Kensky, Phyllis Trible, and others.

I want to thank John McClure, professor of homiletics at Vanderbilt Divinity, who is also a very accomplished music engineer. He was the first to suggest that songs and stories belong together in the pulpit. He convinced me, not an easy task, that I could let my artistic soul shine as a pastor. He's written volumes about this very topic, re-awakening the songwriter in me and helping me to connect songwriting with preaching. He recorded these songs. I want to thank his wife, Annie, for her hospitality, encouragement, and support. Without the two of them, this project would never have happened.

I'm so grateful for the Louisville Institute that funded much of my research, recording, and writing through two generous grants. A very special thanks to Don Richter, whose encouragement, honesty, and belief in this work kept my creative light burning amid the busy work of being a pastor.

I'm very grateful to my friend, esteemed Hebrew Bible scholar, and world-renowned author, Johanna W.H. van Wijk-Bos, who invited me into her fairytale-like home and classroom as the artist in residence at Louisville Presbyterian Seminary. Much of this book took shape as we co-taught a course by the same title. Her wisdom, wit, and friendship have encouraged and driven me to complete this work and to shine it out to the world.

There are so many others to mention whose friendship, support and encouragement have enabled this book to come to life. My literary agent, Rachelle Gardner, has championed this writing. Her wisdom has helped me grow leaps and bounds as an author. Rev. Neelley Hicks, founder of Harper Hill Global and the Women Arise Collective, whose friendship and encouragement have always given me the feeling of possibility. My dear friends Dr. Malinda Davenport-Crisp and Susan Callaway Stein who have walked with me into the journey of creating Beloved Woman, a nonprofit that helps women who are financially disadvantaged to become self-employed. Our work together inspired me to release this as an empowering and healing resource for women. Berywn and Patti Rooks for helping me to experience the wildness of God.

A very special thanks to my editors, Jana Melpolder, Tisha Martin, and Johanna W. H. van Wijk-Bos and my layout editor, Colleen Jones.

I have so much loving gratitude for my parents, who raised me to believe in the power of Bible stories and surrounded me with love, haven, and support. Thank you for believing in me and equipping me with faith.

Finally, I want to thank my partner, husband, and best friend, Patrick J. Woolsey. With unwavering belief, he has taken my hand and walked with me through some of the most challenging work I've ever attempted to do. What an honor to have walked this journey, building lives together in a sacred text.

ABOUT THE AUTHOR

Rev. Sherry Cothran, M.Div, is an ordained United Methodist minister with a past. In the late '90s, she was the lead singer of a popular rock band on Mercury Records, touring with hit acts of the day and living the rock and roll fairytale. Sensing a spiritual calling, she left it all and headed to Vanderbilt Divinity, obtained a Masters of Divinity, and became ordained as a United Methodist minister. While serving as a senior pastor to churches in Nashville and Chattanooga for a decade, Sherry continued to write songs and released her first book, "Tending Angels." The beloved book is a collection of popular stories from her blog in which she shares healing and hope from the "frontlines of heaven and earth." She filmed a music video of the same title that was chosen for three domestic and international film festivals. In this project, her unique presentation of songs and stories was born. Sherry has released four solo CDs and two books. She is the founder and president of the nonprofit Beloved Woman, helping women who are financially disadvantaged to become self-employed. She is an award-winning songwriter whose music has been featured in t.v., film, and radio. Her story has been featured in many publications, including USA Today and interviews, including NPR. She has been the recipient of two grants from the Louisville Institute to develop creative projects for Christian culture and was the Artist in Residence at Louisville Presbyterian Seminary. Her writing has been featured in *Abingdon Women, Ministry Matters, Interpreter Magazine*, and she has been a regular contributor to the homiletics journal, *Good Preacher*. Sherry lives in Chattanooga, TN, with her husband, Patrick, who teaches Bible. Sherry tours regularly, performing, speaking and leading workshops. She is appointed to the nonprofit she founded and oversees, Beloved Woman.

www.sherrycothran.com
www.belovedwoman.org

ENDNOTES

INTRODUCTION

1 Amy-Jill Levine, *The Misunderstood Jew: The Church and the Scandal of the Jewish Jesus*, (New York: Harper Collins, 2006) p. 20.

2 Wilda C. Gafney, *Daughters of Miriam: Women Prophets in Ancient Israel*, (Minneapolis: Augsburg Fortress Press, 2008) p. 1.

3 Elizabeth A. Clark, *Message of the Fathers of the Church: Women in the Early Church*, (Wilmington: Michael Glazier, Inc., 1983) p. 15-17

4 Tertullian, *De Cultu Feminarum*, c. 160–225.

5 Thomas Aquinas, *Summa Theologica I q.92 a.*

6 Augustine of Hippo, *On the Trinity*, 12.7.10

7 Jimmy Carter, *A Call to Action: Women, Religion, Violence, and Power*, (New York: Simon and Schuster, 2014) p. 10.

8 Mary Oliver, *The Summer Day, New and Selected Poems* (Boston: Beacon Press, 1992) p. 143.

9 Clarissa Pinkola Estes, *Women Who Run With the Wolves: Myths and Stories of the Wild. Woman Archetype,* (New York: Ballantine Books, 1992) p. 6.

CHAPTER 1

10 Theda Purdue, *Cherokee Women*, (Lincoln: Nebraska University Press, 1998), p. 38.

11 Ibid., 38.

12 Colin Barras, *Ancient Nomadic Warrior Women May Have Inspired the Mulan Legend*, www.newscientist.com, April 14, 2020).

13 Wilda C. Gafney, *Daughters of Miriam: Women Prophets in Ancient Israel* (Minneapolis: Fortress Press, 2008), p. 190-194.

14 Clarissa Pinkola Estes, *Women Who Run with the Wolves: Myths and Stories of the Wild Woman Archetype* (New York: Ballantine Books, 1992), 6.

15 Bessel Van Der Kolk, *The Body Keeps the Score: Mind, Brain and Body in the Transformation of Trauma*, (Penguin Books, Reprint edition 2015) p. 53.

16 Wilda C. Gafney, *Daughters of Miriam: Women Prophets in Ancient Israel* (Minneapolis: Fortress Press, 2008), p. 193,194.

17 Ibid., x.

18 Ibid., p. 191.

19 Wilda C. Gafney, *Daughters of Miriam: Women Prophets in Ancient Israel* (Minneapolis: Fortress Press, 2008), 153–154.

20 Ibid., 154.

21 Ibid., 154.

CHAPTER 2

22 Johanna W.H. van Wijk-Bos, *The End of the Beginning: Joshua and Judges* (Grand Rapids: Eerdmans Publishing, 2019) p. 220.

23 Bessel Van Der Kolk, *The Body Keeps the Score: Mind, Brain and Body in the Transformation of Trauma*, (Penguin Books, Reprint edition 2015) p. 1.

24 Peter A. Levine, *Waking the Tiger: Healing Trauma*, (Berkeley: North Atlantic Books, 1997) p. 22.

CHAPTER 3

25 Mary Oliver, *The Summer Day, New and Selected Poems* (Boston: Beacon Press, 1992, 143.

26 Martin Buber, *Hasidism and Modern Man*, (Princeton: Princeton University Press, 2015), 66.

27 Rumi, *The Illuminated Rumi*, Author, Michael Green, Translator, Coleman Barks, (Broadway Books, 1997) *p. 31.*

28 Esther Fuchs, *Sexual Politics in the Biblical Narrative: Reading the Hebrew Bible as a Woman* (Sheffield: Sheffield Academic Press, 2003), p. 11.

29 Alice Ogden Bellis, *Helpmates, Harlots and Heroes: Women's Stories in the Hebrew Bible* (Louisville: Westminster John Knox Press, 2007), 61.

CHAPTER 4

30 *Adult Children of Alcoholics* (Torrence: Adult Children of Alcoholics World Service Organization, 2006), p. 194.

31 Johanna W.H. van Wijk-Bos, *The Land and its Kings* (Grand Rapids: Wm. B. Eerdmans, 2020), p. 284.

32 Esther Fuchs, *Sexual Politics in the Biblical Narrative: Reading the Hebrew Bible as a Woman* (Sheffield: Sheffield Academic Press, 2003), p. 12.

33 Wilda C. Gafney, *Daughters of Miriam: Women Prophets in Ancient Israel* (Minneapolis: Fortress Press, 2008) x.

34 Frederick Buechner, *Wishful Thinking* (San Francisco, Harper One, 1973), p. 95.

CHAPTER 5

35 Joseph Campbell, *Myths, Dreams, and Religion* (New York: E.P. Dutton, 1970), p. 52.

CHAPTER 6

36 A.C.A. Handbook Committee, *Adult Children of Alcoholic and Dysfunctional Families* (Torrence: Adult Children of Alcoholics World Service Organization), p. 6.

37 A.C.A Handbook Committee, *Adult Children of Alcoholic and Dysfunctional Families* (Torrence: Adult Children of Alcoholics World Service Organization), p. 60.

38 Thomas Keating, *Divine Therapy and Addiction*, (Brooklyn: Lantern Books, 2011)

CHAPTER 7

39 Elizabeth Bishop, *The Complete Poems* (New York: Farrar, Straus, Giroux, 1984), p. 107.

40 Saint Augustine of Hippo, *On the Trinity*, 12.7.10.

CHAPTER 8

41 Wilda Gafney, *Womanist Midrash: A Reintroduction to Women of the Torah and the Throne*, (Louisville: Westminster John Knox Press, 2017) p. 277.

CHAPTER 9

42 Esther Fuchs, *Sexual Politics in the Biblical Narrative: Reading the Hebrew Bible as a Woman* (Sheffield: Sheffield Academic Press, 2003), p. 12.

43 John Bartlett, *Familiar Quotations*, 10th ed. 1919.

44 Wilda Gafney, *Womanist Midrash: A Reintroduction to Women of the Torah and the Throne*, (Louisville: Westminster John Knox Press, 2017) p. 276.

45 Wilda Gafney, *Womanist Midrash: A Reintroduction to Women of

the Torah and the Throne, (Louisville: Westminster John Knox Press, 2017) p. 276, 277.

46 Wilda Gafney, *Womanist Midrash: A Reintroduction to Women of the Torah and the Throne*, (Louisville: Westminster John Knox Press, 2017) p. 276.

47 Clarissa Pinkola Estes, *Women Who Run with the Wolves: Myths and Stories of the Wild Woman Archetype* (New York: Ballantine Books, 1992) p. 365, 366.

CHAPTER 10

48 Mieke Bal, *Death and Dissymmetry: The Politics of Coherence in the Book of Judges* (Chicago: University of Chicago Press, 1988), p. 231.

Made in the USA
Las Vegas, NV
03 August 2021